# Beck Cultural
# Exchange Center

# The Heat of a
# Red Summer

Robert J. Booker

Beck Cultural Exchange Center

All rights reserved, including the right to reproduce this work
in any form whatsoever without permission in writing
from the Beck Cultural Exchange Center, Inc.,
except for brief passages in connection with a review.

Copyright ©2001 by Robert J. Booker

Cover artwork by Erin Walrath

Interior design by Al Robinson

ALL RIGHTS RESERVED
The Beck Cultural Exchange Center, Inc.
1927 Dandridge Avenue
Knoxville, TN 37915

Manufactured in the United States of America

**Cataloging in Publication Data**
Booker, Robert J.

The Heat of a Red Summer

ISBN: 1-58244-150-2

1. True Crime Chronicle -- 1919.  2.  Maurice Hayes.
3. Race Rioting -- Race Hatred -- Knoxville, Tennessee.

Library of Congress Control Number: 2001089479

*Proceeds to benefit the Beck Cultural Exchange Center*

# Contents

| | |
|---|---|
| Introduction | vii |
| The Hayes Heritage | 1 |
| Maurice Comes of Age | 7 |
| Hayes, the Mature Man, Shapes His Fate | 13 |
| The Day All Hell Broke Loose | 19 |
| The Start of a Fateful Day | 31 |
| Judgment is Rushed | 39 |
| The NAACP Takes an Interest | 49 |
| Some Leading Black Citizens of 1919 | 61 |
| The Slam of the Big Steel Door | 65 |
| His Testimony in Court is Recalled | 81 |
| Beyond the End | 91 |
| Ex-Mayor McCulloch Commits Suicide | 95 |
| Notes Beyond the End | 103 |

# Introduction

He could barely put one foot in front of the other as he was being led down the long, drab hall with a dozen cells on each side. His elderly father held him under the right arm and his church pastor held him under the left. As he half walked and was half carried, he thought to himself, 'How can it be that I, an innocent man, am being taken to my death in the electric chair? God knows that I am not guilty and most men know that I am not guilty of this crime. I know the governor will reprieve me at the last minute," said the pitifully frail Maurice Hayes.

But as the prison entourage reached the door of the death chamber, he could no longer contain himself and he cried out, 'Oh Lord, have mercy! Sheriffs, judges, and the governor have turned their backs on me and I have only you to appeal to. I pray you take my soul in your strong arms and let me abide with you forevermore."

'Bless those thousands who have nobly stood by me, though we stand now in defeat; and forgive those whom the narrowness of prejudice has placed against me. The lash of prejudice has whipped me into the shadows of death. Cleanse the sinful hearts of men who have dipped their fingers in my innocent blood."

"Oh, God, I am innocent of the crime for which I am to die. I pray your forgiveness for all my sins. Give me strength; I want to die bravely. Let me go brave. Bless my friends and forgive my enemies."

Will Hayes, Maurice's father, who had been in the cell with him until that slow march to eternity, embraced his son as Maurice ran his fingers through the old man's gray hair. The two had come a long way together, but now it appeared they would soon be parted forever unless a miracle could stop the wheels of a grave injustice.

Maurice Franklin Hayes had been a man-about-town. He owned a popular nightspot and had gained political influence and made some enemies by dabbling in local politics. For a short time he had served as a deputy sheriff in Knox County.

Although he had dropped out of school in the ninth grade, he had exceptional writing skills and had such a way with words that one might assume he was a college man. Hayes wore the stylish clothes of the day and was meticulous about their care. It is said that he hung the tips of his trouser legs in the top dresser drawer to keep a sharp crease in them. His shoes were always polished to mirrorlike perfection.

Although he was only five feet, eight inches tall, and weighed only 128 pounds, he cut a dashing figure. His dark curly hair and well-chiseled features commanded a second look. He was mild-mannered and spoke in a soft, even tone.

Hayes was popular in his community and was successful in most of his endeavors. By every standard he was far ahead of his time for a black man in 1919. A common rumor was that he was the illegitimate son of the city's white mayor.

The thirty-two-year-old mulatto was king of his world. The handsome, dapper Hayes had money and more women than the

## The Heat of a Red Summer • ix

average man could ever hope to have. Many women all but threw themselves at his feet. Both black and white women found him irresistible. It never occurred to him that he could not have any woman he desired. But the forces in 1919 could not tolerate his behavior with white women and used a legal scheme to curtail his activities—a scheme that left Hayes facing the electric chair, a victim of the heat of a Red Summer.

Hayes had misjudged the tenor of the time in his hometown of Knoxville, Tennessee, in the aftermath of World War I and the attendant racial tensions of the era. He had paid little attention to the threats and taunts of the police officer who warned him about liaisons with white women. And he had not detected the deep anger of the white men who resented his lifestyle.

He was not mindful of the many attacks on white women in their beds by a man or men who were thought to be black. Four of these women were shot and three died. He could not have guessed that these crimes would influence the outcome of his destiny.

Hayes was accustomed to life in a city where racial discord was an aberration. He lived in a southern city that had sympathy with the Union during the Civil War. His city's black population was relatively small and had never witnessed the lynching of a black person.

By most southern standards, it was a liberal city that encouraged blacks to vote immediately after slavery rather than devise schemes to deny them the vote. Blacks began to hold elective office just four years after slavery ended. Knoxville was the only southern city, except for four in Texas, which had black police officers after Reconstruction.

Hayes observed prosperous black businessmen such as Cal Johnson, who owned several saloons in the heart of town and operated the only horse-racing track in the city. He admired the success of William F. Yardley, another black man, who was a successful criminal lawyer and had been a candidate for governor of Tennessee in 1876. Hayes respected Webster L. Porter, who started his newspaper, *The East Tennessee News*, at age seventeen in 1909. And there were several others who caught his attention as successful men and community leaders.

But while the aforementioned men of Hayes's admiration dealt their business on the legal side of the law, much of his dealings developed on the shady side of the law. This, of course, was not uncommon for a number of respected blacks and others who found different avenues to success. It was a time where certain activities were tolerated by the power structure if they did not spill over into the larger community.

So it was in this context that Maurice Hayes was allowed to dabble in various enterprises and to prosper and eventually be taken to the bar of justice (injustice?) for his activities.

Born in Knoxville on April 12, 1887, Hayes enjoyed the life of two worlds without realizing the inherent dangers that lay ahead. Active in politics and social circles, he didn't understand the bounds in the romancing of white women. Although he thought his liaisons were secret, they were more public than he realized, and the whispers began to get louder.

But the summer of 1919, known as Red Summer, would graphically show him the "black man's place." Accused of murdering a white woman, set upon by a lynch mob, and convicted in two trials, Hayes became the center of unwanted national attention. Ironically, the Knoxville branch of the National Association for the Advancement of Colored People (NAACP) was organized just four days before Hayes's arrest.

Knoxville's Red Summer was just one of at least twenty-five

that occurred in cities throughout the country that summer. There were eighty-three lynchings in those cities. At least ten of those victims were veterans returning from the war; several were in uniform.

W.E.B. DuBois had declared in the spring issue of the *NAACP Crisis Magazine*, "We return. We return from fighting. We return fighting. Make way for democracy! We saved it in France, and by the Great Jehovah, we will save it in the U.S.A. or know the reason why!"

James Weldon Johnson, a prominent official of the NAACP coined the term "Red Summer" because of the bloodied streets of the riot-torn cities of the United States. He noted that the injustices and harassment were not only the tools of the mobs, but of local, state, and federal officials as well.

Several black leaders and publications that protested prejudice and injustice were labeled subversive by Attorney General A. Mitchell Palmer in 1919. A. Philip Randolph, the editor of the *Messenger* was arrested for news items in his publication. Justice Department officials called upon NAACP leader DuBois to explain the purposes of the NAACP. Other horrors may have been perpetrated by some local and state governments to curtail black protests of injustice.

This was the backdrop for the story of Maurice Hayes and the people who influenced his life. It presents the overtones and undertones of the time, which led to his downfall. It dramatically shows how southern courtroom injustice taught black men a lesson to keep them in their place.

There was no effort by Hayes's prosecutors to contain their racial prejudices in presenting their case. There likewise was no protest of these tactics by the defense as its client was being railroaded for a crime he did not commit.

The legal charade was played to the hilt with a parade of witnesses for both sides, but the outcome was already set in stone. One of the prosecuting attorneys on several occasions referred to Hayes in the courtroom as 'The nigger who committed the crime," or 'The nigger who was on the scene." The defense never challenged such inflammatory language.

There was even an effort to make the defense position more tenable by placing two black lawyers on the team. Although they were very able lawyers in their own right and had represented the black community well in less volatile issues, they had nothing to say at the Hayes trial and had no obvious impact on its outcome. It is not likely that this charade fooled anyone in the black community.

Such shenanigans were not new for the city of Knoxville. Certain blacks had always been placed in interesting positions to placate the black community whether they succeeded or not. City leaders believed more in the right perception than in the right thing. But these appointed leaders were more often tolerated than respected.

Although Knoxville blacks had been free from the physical chains of slavery for fifty-four years in 1919, they were not so free from psychological slavery and the chicanery of white political leaders. The city and county Jim Crow laws were a constant reminder. Most blacks knew their place and stayed in it.

In 1919, Knoxville Colored High School graduated a class of thirty-two students. Over the years, several of them became prominent citizens, especially in the field of education, yet the city of Knoxville required them to have only ten years of classroom work before finishing high school.

So, even though Hayes left school in the ninth grade, his formal education was almost completed. It wasn't until 1935 that the school system added the twelfth grade in the local black high school. An eleventh grade had been added in 1921.

It was so interesting to see how comparatively "liberal" Knoxville could be on one hand with its black citizens and yet keep them on a short leash with the other. With the possible exception of a nominal poll tax, there was nothing to keep blacks from voting. They were not only encouraged to vote, but allowed to run for office.

The first black, Isaac Gammon, a railroad worker, was elected to the city board of aldermen in 1869. Melvin Gentle, a shoemaker, was elected to the Knox County Court in 1870 and served until 1876. He also was elected to the board of alderman from 1875 to 1877.

In 1866, Gentle was elected president of the State Convention of Colored Citizens which passed resolutions demanding the right to vote and other rights. He also became the first black deputy sheriff of Knox County in 1879. He was no "handkerchief head" and was respected by both blacks and whites.

The state of Tennessee had no laws prohibiting slaves from learning to read or write. Many of them were taught by youngsters in the households of their owners. Before the Civil War, Reverend Thomas Humes, the rector of St. John's Episcopal Church, taught free blacks as a part of his calling.

In 1881, the city board of education chose a black Yale graduate to be principal of Austin School to develop it into a first-class institution for black students. The principal, John W. Manning, went to Wilburforce and received his master's degree in 1889. By 1900, he had assembled a competent, dedicated faculty, and had developed a curriculum comparable to that of the white high schools.

Manning's school had been started by a white woman, Emily L. Austin, in 1879, and he was able to graduate the first tenth-grade class in 1888, the year before he received his master's degree.

But 1888 also showed the dark side of Knoxville in race relations. When Reverend Job Childs Lawrence, a black, was elected to the city school board, he never was able to take his seat. Although he was the pastor of Shiloh Presbyterian Church and was elected to his position by the board of aldermen, he could not serve.

The fight against Lawrence began with the agitation of two newspapers, the *Knoxville Daily Tribune* and the *Knoxville Sentinel*. They traded barbs about him and printed letters from parents against him. In the Tribune on February 2, 1888, one father wrote, 'Parents of children in schools, especially girls, should view the pending danger in its true light, and appreciate the full significance of the situation."

All kinds of questions continued to arise. Would Lawrence have control over white schools? Was there a clear danger of race-mixing in the schools? Would he have access to the girls' locker room? The clear response was that parents should rise up and invalidate the election.

Reverend Lawrence was never able to attend a school board meeting. They were always unannounced and held in secret places. He took his case to the state Supreme Court, but lost when the court ruled that he did not get a majority of the aldermanic vote because one alderman had tendered a blank vote which could not be construed as a positive one. So, in essence, the vote was four for and four against. Lawrence's election never was.

No black was appointed or elected to the school board until

## The Heat of a Red Summer • xv

eighty-one years later. In fact, by 1912, city fathers had a change of heart and blacks no longer were welcome in public office. The only visible blacks in authority were in the police department.

It appears that the local newspapers delighted in denigrating black citizens. They not only attacked the character and mores of blacks in their pages, but made fun of their weight and shapes. It was not uncommon to read that 'Heavyset Pearl Smith, Negro of Patton Street, was arrested for public drunkenness," or that 'James Turner, stumpy Negro of New Street, was found beaten by unknown assailants." The black business district was oftentimes described as 'Little Harlem."

*The Journal and Tribune*, a daily newspaper, almost never carried a positive story about blacks. In fact, nearly all of the stories about blacks were of their being lynched in other parts of the state and throughout the South. When blacks in Knoxville were mentioned, it carried stories about domestic fights, gambling, or cocaine raids.

One story described the raid on a 'cocaine school frequented by from fifty to one hundred Negroes. The raid was made at the building of 315 Central Street."That address was just a few doors from the black high school.

*The article continued,*

> Constable Chanaberry took possession of the paraphernalia of the schoolrooms consisting of some 10 or 15 boxes of cocaine and about half that number of needles. The cocaine was put up in small tin boxes and these sold at 25 cents a piece.
>
> Constable Chanaberry says that he found the cocaine lying all about the room, some in the bedclothes, others in parts of the room, the 'scholars' using the floor. He destroyed much of the 'dope' by kicking it with his feet, wasting several dollars worth in

*this way. The rest he carried to the office of Squire Knabe to be used for evidence in convicting the defendants.*

*Constable Chanaberry states that the 'school' has been running for three or four weeks at this place and neighbors have complained of all night noises, brawls, and continuous fighting. There are schools in other parts of the city.*

*The Negroes call the deadly needles 'guns' and when they are filled with cocaine, they say the 'guns' are 'loaded' and several of them pierce their flesh with the needle points and insert the deadly drug.*

*The trouble begins with the happy stage; when it wears off it starts the 'scholars' to fighting among themselves. This continues until physical exhaustion and lassitude ensues from the reaction and effects of the drug.*

*Chanaberry states that the Negro, Arthur Steele, appears to be the worst victim of the effects of the continued use of the drug. His body is literally covered with sores where the needle has been used. So often has he used the drug that the ordinary injection has little effect on him and he has resorted to the method of using it in his eyes, which have become almost blinded as a result.*

One telling example of racial insensitivity in the *Daily Journal and Tribune* was its choice of popular music of the month. It published several songs with words and music, such as the following:

*'Little Dark Brown Lou"*
*Way down in Alabama where de colored people dwell,*
*Lived a little coffee colored coon,*
*He done got spoon-ey on a dusky little belle,*
*A girl he meant to wed right soon.*
*But this little nigger was jealous as could be,*

*And so she loved a little joke to play,*
*When she wouldn't talk to him, this he always used to say*
*Oh, Lou, tell me if you do, love your little honey anymore?*
*You is just de neatest, deed you is the sweetest*
*Girl dat I ever saw! Lordy, Lordy, Lordy, come sis*
*Give your man a kiss, 'cause he won't be happy till you do*
*Honey, don't deceive me, say dat you believe me,*
*Little Dark Brown Lou.*

*The Daily Journal and Tribune* either didn't realize or didn't care how offensive its music or comments were. Yet, these uncomplimentary descriptions and comments obviously influenced many white readers who felt it all right to view blacks in such a derogatory light.

In November 1881, Frederick Douglass, the noted abolitionist, visited Knoxville College and made a public speech at Staub's Opera House. The place was packed with both black and white citizens. He spoke for two hours while a driving rain poured outside.

Perhaps the most interesting thing about Douglass's visit was the fact that the host committee put him up at the Hattie House, which was Knoxville's premier hotel at the time. This was reported in the newspapers, but not one complaint was heard. How could that be?

It seems that Knoxville was open to playing host to 'special"Negroes. Those who had made a name for themselves and were respected on the national and international scene were welcome. But local celebrities could not apply for such amenities.

Although the local papers took great pains not to mix black achievements in white society columns, they made an effort to recognize black achievements in special editions. They would print a whole page highlighting the "Advancement Of Our Colored Citizens." Such pages would focus on preachers and educators. They gave sketches of church histories and school activities.

Government officials and the newspapers made blacks mindful of their place in society and there could be no doubt where that place was. Unfortunately, Maurice Hayes had forgotten and he would have hell to pay for his lapse in memory.

# The Hayes Heritage

Maurice Hayes's mother had disappeared early in his life. He was too young to remember her, but older people in the community could give a compelling description of her. They knew Sarah Lou Smith, a petite, brown-skinned woman who did day work for several white families in West Knoxville.

She came to Knoxville with her mother's sister and her uncle from some place in Georgia in 1882 when she was thirteen years old. The aunt and uncle began rearing her when her mother died of tuberculosis.

The first house they occupied was on Depot Street. Her aunt's husband, James Garrett, eventually went to work for the Knoxville Gas Company. Her Aunt Lucy did day work for several prominent white families and often took Sarah to assist with various chores.

By the time she was seventeen, Sarah Lou had become a striking young woman. She was not much over five feet tall with large brown eyes and shoulder length, black hair. She had attended the Austin School on Central Street but dropped out after the seventh grade.

She decided that it was easier to do housework for the white folk than to worry about classes in Latin, Greek, and geometry.

Besides, she enjoyed taking care of her employer's children and taking charge of the household chores.

Sarah was well liked by her employers, Mr. and Mrs. David Gammon, who tried to convince her to go back to school. She was a popular member of her youth group at Mount Olive Baptist Church on Patterson Street. The pastor, Reverend Maskins, encouraged her to sing in the junior choir and share her beautiful voice.

She seemed to have little interest in the young men who tried to woo her. It appeared that she was bored with the usual hayrides, picnics, and ice cream socials where people her age mixed and mingled. In 1886, she celebrated her eighteenth birthday quietly at home with her aunt and uncle.

As a maid and general house girl in the elegant home of the Gammons, she had the opportunity to observe Knoxville's elite. On occasions, she was asked to serve at special parties for other families.

One of those other families was the McCullochs. Their son, John, was celebrating his twentieth birthday and Sarah Lou was asked to serve them that evening. Young Mr. McCulloch was immediately smitten by the charm and good looks of his bronze servant. That evening led to several other invitations for Sarah Lou to be of service in the McCulloch household.

Although interracial couples were a rarity in Knoxville and the custom was frowned upon, some co-mixing did exist. While it was common knowledge in a few cases, most liaisons were kept private.

This was the case with Sarah Lou and John McCulloch. But after several months, sharp eyes and ears began to catch a connection of more than employer and housekeeper. Even a little gossip began to circulate in the black community. Most people, however, attributed it to envy. When Sarah Lou's son was born a year later, suspicions were confirmed.

The child had very light skin at birth and could have been mistaken for a white baby. He had curly, dark brown hair and a keen nose. Since his mother had a medium brown complexion, the natural conclusion was that his father was white.

Although there were light-skinned black men who could have fathered the child, it was not likely. Sarah Lou had not shown interest in any of the fellows who sought her attention. In fact, people thought her to be a good Christian girl who had no time for boys.

And perhaps she didn't, but the suave, successful John McCulloch lived in the kind of world of which she dared not dream. He treated her like a lady and not just a house servant. He showered her with praise for her housework, and often told her of her good looks.

He was a man of wit and charm who could use just the right words. "I don't see any difference in colored and white people," he told her. "It's just our way of life down here that keeps us separated. You are one of the finest women I know."

Sarah Lou had never heard that kind of talk from a white man before. In fact, she had never heard it from any mature man at all. She had heard all the jive from the boys in her neighborhood, and she had heard some of the girls discuss their experiences, but she had no desire to take part in such meaningless relationships.

With John McCulloch she felt like a real woman. He knew how to stroke and caress her. His kisses stirred the fire in her loins, and in his arms she could let herself go. She knew the consequences, but those precious moments were worth it.

During the next thirty years, McCulloch, who became the

mayor of Knoxville, would play an interesting role in the life of his love child. Though never admitting paternity, it was obvious that he was interested in his son's welfare and assisted him in his endeavors. He also bailed him out of serious trouble.

Born in Knoxville on December 7, 1868, John was the son of James H. and Mary McCulloch. He graduated from Bell House School and worked in the office of a wholesale furniture company for more than four years. During this time he met Sarah Lou.

In 1890, he left the furniture company and headed the city's finance department. He became head cashier and later, president of the Second National Bank of Knoxville.

In 1900, he married Miss Lena Dunlap, one of the city's leading young ladies. In 1915, he was elected mayor of Knoxville.

With his future endeavors in mind, McCulloch could hardly have afforded to have it generally known that he had fathered a child out of wedlock, let alone a black child. He had to make a tough decision.

By the time Sarah Lou's son, Maurice, was one year old, McCulloch had convinced her to move to Detroit and leave the boy with a childless black couple, Mr. and Mrs. Will Hayes, where he would be well cared for.

Sarah Lou, realizing that there could be no semblance of life with McCulloch and that she could no longer work in that household, knew that her life had changed. Fearing that life for her could become unpleasant in both the black and white communities once the word became common knowledge, she agreed to McCulloch's terms. Although she loved her son deeply, she knew his chances for a better life lay under the influences of his father.

She left for Detroit in June 1888 and was not heard from again. She had accepted McCulloch's offer to assist with her upkeep until she was well situated. She never again contacted her aunt and uncle.

# Maurice Comes of Age

Sarah Lou's son, Maurice, was a bright young boy who excelled in baseball and was quite athletic. He was one of only eight boys who made the seventh-grade honor roll at Austin School in 1903.

By the time young Hayes had reached the age of fifteen, people realized he was different. His dashing good looks, his athleticism, unusually good vocabulary, and his ability to assert himself made people take notice.

As a baby he had been placed in the home of twenty-three-year-old William Hayes and his wife, Hazel, who adopted him and gave him their last name. Living at 530 Campbell Street, Will Hayes worked for the Spiro Processing Company, which made vinegar and cider. He had begun his employment there in 1884.

The Hayeses were members of the Logan Temple A.M.E. Zion Church where William was a trustee, and Hazel served on the Number Two Usher Board. Both were devoted church members and they took young Maurice along and established his membership.

For young Maurice, living on Campbell Street did not provide the best surroundings. While he had a mother and father who were productive citizens who gave him love and provided him with a relatively comfortable life, the outside influences strongly beckoned to him.

The family had to deal with the various whiskey houses, floating crap games, and bawdy houses. They were always plagued by the spring overflow of First Creek that forced them out of their home. There were constant fights and murders, and turmoil from people who lived on the edge of the law. The Hayes's home was in the heart of the Bottom, one of the city's most notorious neighborhoods.

Before 1913, it was even difficult for churches to survive in that neighborhood. St. Paul Independent Methodist Church, one of the oldest black churches in the city, decided to build an edifice on Campbell Street near the turn of the century. Conditions were so bad the congregation relocated at the corner of Condon and Patton.

Young Hayes was well aware of his surroundings and learned to blend in. Since he was well liked and trusted by some of the operators outside of and on the edge of the law, they had him run errands for them. He delivered pints of whiskey to some of the city's well-heeled citizens in affluent neighborhoods. He sometimes delivered payoff money to police officials.

But early on, Hayes ran into serious trouble. At age seventeen, in 1907, he killed teenager John 'Shorty" Boyd in an argument over a crap game. Hayes claimed Boyd was cheating and when he challenged him he pulled out an ice pick. He claimed he shot Boyd in self-defense.

He was convicted of manslaughter in the Knox County Juvenile Court, but was pardoned by the governor. This was, perhaps, the first time he felt his biological father's influence in a major way. Had it not been for the intervention of John McCulloch, he was penitentiary bound. Instead, his record was expunged and no evidence of the trial exists.

The Hayes's neighborhood had pockets of extreme poverty and elements of pseudo-wealth. There were those who did not have regular jobs and did piecework and scavenging to make ends meet. They often got food from the trash cans at nearby wholesale food companies along the Southern Railway tracks. The food was generally clean and good, but the packaging was damaged and it had to be discarded. Many were able to survive by having small gardens and raising chickens.

On the other hand, those who had ready access to cash were the bootleggers who sold moonshine whiskey, and the butter-n-egg people who ran the numbers business. Although most of these people could in no way be considered rich, they could afford to lend small amounts of money and live more comfortably than most other people in the neighborhood.

The main structure in the neighborhood was Heiskell Elementary School at 903 Campbell Street. Young Hayes attended Heiskell School in the first and second grades before being transferred to the Austin School some seven blocks from his home.

He began his first year of school in the brand new Heiskell School, which was dedicated on November 11, 1897. Named for Samuel G. Heiskell, the mayor of the city, it was the first new public school ever built for black children in Knoxville. It is ironic that Heiskell, known as a champion for black rights near the turn of the century, would later be the prosecuting attorney against Hayes in a murder trial.

Maurice grew up with the sights, sounds, and smells of his

neighborhood in the Bottom. (It was called that because it was generally in a low-lying area.) Bounded on the south by Vine Avenue, the north by the Southern Railroad tracks, the west by Central Street, and the east by Preston Street, it was usually ravaged by First Creek during the spring rains.

Since the creek channel was shallow and often was clogged with debris, two or three days of rain drove it beyond its banks to plague nearby streets. It was not uncommon to see residents of Georgia, Paddleford, Water, Willow, Campbell, Florida, and other streets in the area evacuated by the Red Cross.

During the summer, however, the creek became a prime recreational attraction. Hayes and other boys went skinny-dipping in it just off Willow Street behind the Knox-City Iron Works. From their swimming hole they could see the trestle that carried the train tracks to various businesses in the area. They would sometimes hop the slow-moving train and ride for blocks as it meandered to its destination.

The huffing, puffing steam engine entered the Bottom by crossing Jackson Avenue at First Creek just east of Heiskell School and made its way under the Georgia Street Bridge heading toward downtown Knoxville. It rode a spur track which connected with the main Southern tracks near what is now the Bill Meyer Baseball Stadium.

On it way to the Bottom it serviced the Standard Knitting Mills, several coal companies, and other businesses as it crossed the trestle under the Magnolia Avenue Bridge. It passed the North Star Ice Company before reaching Jackson Avenue.

Maurice Hayes found hopping the trains and dodging the railroad dicks exciting. He kept up that dangerous activity until he witnessed the tragic accident of fourteen-year-old James Wilson, who missed a step trying to hop a train and fell under the wheels. He lost his left leg just below the knee. Hayes literally lost his stomach that day and never hopped a train again.

The train also hauled live cattle to and from the East Tennessee Stockyards. There were large holding pens near the corner of Willow and Central where buyers and sellers dealt in livestock. Hayes often saw women from the community bring their buckets to milk the cows waiting to be sold. He also experienced some of the more unpleasant odors of the Bottom there.

One of the rituals of the Bottom was to get rid of chinches. Also known as bedbugs, which survived by sucking human blood as one slept at night. It was not unusual for one to wake up the next day and find his undershirt red with bloodstains where the varmints had gotten their fill.

To combat those creatures, some people sprayed insecticide on their bedding. Others took the springs off the bed and burned torches of newspaper under the coils to kill the bugs and their eggs. Some placed kerosene-filled coasters under the legs of the bed to keep the insects from crawling into the bed. Of course, none of these efforts was foolproof.

There were also the sights, sounds, and festival atmosphere of the Friday night or Saturday night fish fry at Mt. Calvary Baptist Church at the corner of Jackson and Kentucky. In order to raise money for certain organizations within the church, the ladies would bring their cast-iron skillets and buckets of lard and make a fire for the event.

Most of the fish they sold in their sandwiches came from the Tennessee River. Carp and catfish were the main types to be caught near the mouth of the East Tennessee Packing Company sewers located just east of the Gay Street Bridge.

By the time Mt. Calvary was established, Maurice Hayes

was in his early twenties and a man of visible means. He delighted in buying fish sandwiches for some of the drooling youngsters whose eyes sparkled in the light of the glowing embers as the women turned the fish in the sizzling grease.

# HAYES, THE MATURE MAN, SHAPES HIS FATE

As Hayes grew into manhood, he had experienced more than most men twice his age. He fully knew and understood the ways of Knoxville's underworld. He worked with the players, knew their customers, and had rapport with those who operated the government. He even worked on the side of the law for a while.

In 1916, at the age of twenty-nine, he became a deputy sheriff during the administration of Sheriff John Petway. It was the time of the fee grabber system when deputies were paid according to the number of arrests they made and the amount of fines collected. It was also a time when officers were not trained in the law, but could attract votes for the sheriff.

The sheriff also thought Hayes would be valuable in making certain inroads into the black community underworld. But, Hayes had not reformed and was not likely to. He had too many friends who depended on his 'Ignorance" of their activities.

After only a year with the sheriff's department, Hayes decided that going into business for himself would be more profitable and safer. In 1917, he opened a small nightclub at 324 Jackson Avenue.

With secondhand tables and chairs, the establishment was well appointed. A large mirror behind the counter reflected the soft drinks and cream brews which lined the back bar. The place could accommodate forty people sitting at one time, which included the seats at the bar.

Although the state of Tennessee had outlawed the sale of liquor eight years earlier, in 1909, Knoxville still had ready access to all the booze it desired. Liquor flowed in Hayes's Stroll Café nightclub as if he could tap the source faucet. The leading bootleggers were his friends, the people who had money were his customers, and the powers that be were his guardian angels.

Because of his connections and personality, Hayes ran a profitable business. His stepfather, Will Hayes, joined him in the business. Although the older Hayes had worked for Spiro's for some thirty-three years and hated to give up his job, the fumes from the vinegar and other products had taken a toll on his lungs.

Hayes's nightclub built a good reputation for having great pan-fried catfish served with pinto beans, cole slaw, and fried cornbread. It did a brisk lunch business. Many white people who worked in the area ordered carryout lunches. A few who felt comfortable and feared no reprisals sat and ate on the premises.

In addition to his father, Hayes employed a bartender/waiter, a cook, a dishwasher, and two hostesses who doubled as waitresses as the crowd warranted. Hayes and his father made a good living in the business and sought various ways to make it even better and more popular.

The greatest attraction at the Stroll Café was the dance floor where many of the new dance fads of the day could be enjoyed. Hayes's two hostesses, Margo and Stella, were recent transplants from Chicago and New York who knew the ropes and the latest dance steps as well. They could demonstrate and teach the turkey trot, kangaroo dip, the snake, and the maxixe, which were the rage.

The shapely tan hostesses were eager to crank up the gramophone during the weekdays and show their stuff. They played the tunes of Sophie Tucker, Grace Kerns, Marion Harris, Bill Murray, and others. One of the favorite dances was the syncopated cakewalk. Elements of the Jones Cornet Band provided live music for some occasions. Other pianists and banjoists often sat in.

Although most of the artists who performed there were local entertainers, sometimes big names made an appearance. One of those was blues legend Bessie Smith, who was in town to do a show with the Silas Green tent show. Although she had not yet begun to make records, she enjoyed wide popularity through stage, cabaret, and tent show appearances.

During her appearance in Knoxville in 1917, Miss Smith had just finished a gig at the Paradise Café in Atlantic City, New Jersey. She had earlier done some shows with Silas Green. She popped into Hayes's place to get some local flavor and was at first reluctant to perform, but the crowd would not take no for an answer.

A local musician accompanied her on the piano as she sang "Alexander's Ragtime Band," "Pretty Baby," and "You Made Me Love You." Although she was delighted with the response of the crowd, she refused to do an encore and settled down for a few drinks. Patrons were delightfully shocked when she ordered that, "The joint be locked up to let the whiskey flow!"

The order sent Hayes dashing to his secret liquor stash in a nearby abandoned building to fill it. He and two of his friends returned with enough to last until the wee hours.

Bessie Smith's visit to the Stroll Café served to make the place even more popular. As the word spread on the street, would-be customers wondered which famous star would pay a visit next. Many came to see. Business continued to grow.

Maurice's successful business and good looks attracted women by the dozen, but he was not a vain man. He was not driven by sex or curiosity to accommodate those who desired his attention. He liked the company of good-looking women, but had no intention, for the most part, to bed them. Naturally, he accommodated a few, but it was because of his desires and not theirs.

In the course of his business transactions across the city, he caught the eye of several young white women who made themselves available. That taboo was just too enticing to resist. This led to several flings with white women and naturally created ill feelings among black women who felt cheated.

The really dangerous side of the coin, however, was the knowledge of those in the white community who became aware of these assignations. City police officer Tony Black was especially agitated and incensed. He made it a point to stop by Hayes's place to register his protest in no uncertain terms. Said he, "You little yellow bastard, if I ever catch you with your britches down with a white woman, I will send your ass to the penitentiary."

When respected black attorney George McDade made a customary visit to the city jail one morning, he encountered Officer Black ranting about the activities of Hayes. He told McDade, "The cute little son of a bitch helped two colored boys get away who had taken a white man's money to buy liquor. I want to see his ass in jail."

On June 30, 1917, Maurice Hayes decided to settle down. He

married twenty-eight-year-old Maude Davis. But, in reality, he did not settle down. His dealings with white women seemed to increase.

Word began to spread of his activities and his business began to suffer. Police raided his establishment unmercifully and his patrons feared to venture there. His wife, Maude, after two years of marriage, could stand it no longer. She packed her bags and moved back to Chicago. The Stroll Caféclosed its doors in July 1919.

The summer of 1919 was very volatile. There was unrest all over. Black soldiers from World War I were making utterances against the segregated society to which they had returned. Authorities were anxious about the rash of attacks on white women by an unknown person who was thought to be black.

The public was in an uproar, demanding that the perpetrator be caught. Officials were frustrated and looking in all directions for leads and evidence. The usually staid, complacent Knoxville population had been pushed to the edge.

# THE DAY ALL HELL BROKE LOOSE

The murder of Bertha Langley, a white woman, on August 30, 1919, lit the fuse for the greatest upheaval in the history of the city since the Civil War. Asleep in bed with her cousin, Ora Smith, Mrs. Langley was shot in her home at 1216 Eighth Avenue at 2:20 a.m. Miss Smith told investigators that the assailant was a black man. She could offer no further description.

When police officer Tony Black, who hated Hayes, heard of the murder, he rode in the paddy wagon from the city jail to the scene of the crime with black patrolman Jim Smith. On the way he told Smith, "That God-damned Maurice Hayes killed that woman."

After visiting the crime scene, Smith, Black, and two other officers went to the Hayes home at 213 Humes Street, rousted him out of bed, and arrested him. They demanded to see his gun and smelled it to see if it had recently been fired. Detecting no odor, they replaced it in a drawer. They later picked it up again and took it in for evidence. Hayes was taken to jail.

Word spread quickly that a black man accused of murdering a white woman was being held in the Knox County Jail. Some extremists who heard of Hayes's relations with white women whipped discussions into a frenzy. They contacted their buddies across the city and urged them to meet at the county jail for a necktie party.

A necktie party in Knoxville, Tennessee? How did things get to that state? Thoughts like that were never had and words like those were never spoken before. Even when nineteen-year-old Jackson Staples was arrested for raping a white woman in Knox County on February 18, 1890, there was no outcry for his neck.

Staples professed his innocence, but the jury found him guilty and he was legally hanged at the Knox County Jail. The only crowd to gather in the Staples case was the 1,500 people who turned out to witness the execution. The crowd was so large Sheriff Tom Holloway decided against having a public hanging or viewing the body afterward.

There are other such stories with graphic details of black men brutalizing white women. All were hanged through the legal system without a hint from a lynch mob.

It would seem that in the summer of 1919, cooler heads would have prevailed. There were no radical outcries for social justice from the black community and Klan activities there were minimal. Knoxville appeared to be proud of its race relations.

There were no elected black officials during that time. Dr. Henry Morgan Green had served on the board of aldermen until 1912. The last county court member was Samuel Maples, who left office in 1897. None had served on the school board or in the state legislature.

There were at least four black policemen, who included Charles Redmond, Dave Saunders, John Singleton, and James Smith. They had the same arrest powers as white officers. This was in contrast to some other larger southern cities such as Atlanta, Memphis, Nashville, and Chattanooga, which did not hire black officers until 1948. New Orleans followed in 1950.

Black Knoxvillian Cora E. Burke was heralded as the national president of the Court of Calanthe. For the first time women

## The Heat of a Red Summer • 21

would be allowed to vote in the city elections on September 6, 1919. Groups such as the Acacia Rose Circle, a group of black women organized in 1902, helped with the registration of black women for the occasion.

Things seemed so normal and calm that no one would have expected a necktie party to take place in Knoxville.

Sheriff Bob Cade knew differently. He took the organizers of the party seriously and made plans of his own. To protect the welfare of his prisoner, he devised a plan to sneak Hayes to Chattanooga for safekeeping.

Borrowing a wig and dress from one of his employees, he dressed Hayes as a woman, spirited him to a waiting car, and drove to the Southern Depot in Concord, Tennessee, some fifteen miles away, to catch the train. The sheriff, Hayes, and two deputies waited at the depot for nearly three hours for train number four which stopped according to the telegraphic orders it received.

Since Hayes's disguise was removed and he was in handcuffs, a small crowd gathered to look, but it is not certain that the people knew who he was. He was offered food by the officers, but he said he was not hungry. When the train finally arrived, he boarded it with the sheriff and a special agent of the Southern Railway. They arrived in Chattanooga at 6:00 p.m.

Not realizing that Hayes was no longer in the Knox County Jail, the mob began to gather shortly after 4:00 p.m. It continued to grow until 7:00 p.m. when the streets surrounding the jail were completely blocked and excitement was at a fever pitch.

As word spread the crowd continued to grow and shout, 'Give us that nigger Hayes!" Efforts by the jailers to quiet the crowd were fruitless. They even allowed three committees from the crowd to search the jail to show Hayes was not there, but that made no difference.

They demanded that the doors be thrown open and that Hayes be brought forward. At 7:45 p.m., someone fired a shot into the air signaling the time to rush the jail. Other shots followed and stones were thrown until every window in the jail was broken.

'We mean business,"shouted one; 'Give us the nigger, now!" The first storming party rushed the main door at 7:50 using a large timber as a battering ram. The door wouldn't fall. They tried unsuccessfully to batter down a smaller door. It, too, could not be knocked down.

Finally, the mob used a heavy timber to batter the double windows on the Hill Street side of the building. After knocking them completely out of the brickwork, scores of angry, shouting men rushed inside as more shots were fired by someone in the crowd.

Deputy Sheriff Earl Hall, seeing that the window was out and that it made an entrance larger than an average door, made a valiant effort to stop the mob, but was overpowered. The mob then turned its attention to forcing open an outside door to let others in. Some men used a battering ram for fifteen minutes without success. One man finally took out his pistol and with two blasts destroyed the lock and the door was opened.

The crowd, totaling hundreds of people, attempted to force its way into the narrow space which could hardly accommodate fifty. For hours they rambled through the jail hearing false reports that Hayes had been found.

After the leaders of the mob entered a storage room where a large quantity of confiscated whiskey was kept, the end of a 16-gallon keg was smashed and pint cups from the kitchen were provided for the men to drink it. When that was consumed, the men and boys in the crowd rushed for a large number of quart bottles and took them from the jail.

Sixteen prisoners were turned loose. Several of them had

been convicted of first-degree murder and one was under sentence to be electrocuted. Among them were Ehude Fellows, Charles Paul, Charles Ryan, and C.W. White. White, ironically, was a black man from Blount County who had murdered a white man and had been sentenced to die.

Only after state troops arrived was any kind of order restored. By the time the mob cleared out, damage to the jail totaled more than $50,000.

Now, half drunk and crazed with the excitement of their effort, there was no stopping the mob. 'Let's go down to Little Harlem and kill every nigger we see," said a loud voice. "Yeah, let's go,"shouted the mob in near unison.

Upon leaving the jail heading for the black business district some six blocks away, the mob thought it should be better armed. Several men broke into Kenner's Pawn Shop at 125 Gay Street and stole more than twenty pistols.

Another bunch took fifty guns and pistols from Uncle Sam's Loan Company. A crowd of fifty or so broke into the S.B. Luttrell Hardware Store and looted it of firearms. Another group smashed the doors of C.M. McClung Company and took whatever could be of use in their mission.

One other group broke into the W.W. Woodruff Hardware Company and took fifteen or twenty guns of the finest quality. They also took ammunition and knives. The damage to the stores was more than $10,000.

After the pillage of the stores and shops, the crowd split into several squads fanning out into various black sections of town. The largest group, however, continued on to Vine and Central, the heart of the black business community.

After a full night of shootings and altercations at the corner of Vine and Central and sporadic confrontations in other parts of the city, the Sunday morning *Journal and Tribune* of August 31, 1919, reported in headlines: 'BLOODY RIOTS FOLLOW ATTACK ON JAIL; FIVE KNOWN DEAD; MANY ARE WOUNDED."

The article continued,

> At midnight serious rioting began at Vine and Central Street and national guardsmen were rushed there from the jail. A Negro was killed at that point just before the troops arrived. A machine gun was turned on a crowd of Negroes who approached the troops. Several fell.
>
> First Lieutenant James W. Payne of Providence, Kentucky, a regular army officer attached to the Fourth Tennessee as an instructor, was killed when he accidentally stepped in the line of fire. The others wounded were shot down in the general fight at Vine and Central or in isolated contests.
>
> The known dead are Lieutenant James Payne, _____ Henderson, Jim Henson, Negro, and two unidentified Negroes. The known wounded are policeman James Benson, shot in the leg; deputy sheriff Clowers, shot in the leg; Gid Thomas; _____ Potter; E.B. Henderson, motorman, shot twice in lower back.
>
> W.B. Morton, policeman, shot in right leg; Fred Johnson, shot in lower abdomen; W.B. Clapp, shot in right arm; Grant Odell, shot in ankle; and George D. Spurgeon, shot in the head.

The article goes on to say that, "At least five men were killed; a half-dozen were wounded seriously and a score or more were injured in rioting Saturday night and early Sunday morning."

Before the mob arrived, the men of the black community were preparing a defense. They were well aware of the action of the mob at the Knox County Jail and were anticipating its next move. They knew that their businesses at the corner of Vine and Central would be the most vulnerable targets.

By 11:00 p.m., while the mob was breaking into and pillaging the hardware stores and pawn shops for various weapons, more than one hundred black men gathered in the business district to make their stand. They came with a collection of pistols, rifles, and mostly, shotguns. Since some of them were avid hunters of small game, they had weapons and ammunition.

For some twenty-five years, the area had been known as the city's main black business district. It was the place where most blacks went to socialize. Saturday was the main night to socialize in what the daily newspapers called Little Harlem.

On the northeast corner of Vine and Central was the Famous Building. It was a four-story building which housed the offices of several black physicians. There was a large grocery store on the street floor and a dance hall on an upper floor. It also provided space and a meeting hall for large and small group meetings.

The Gem Theater sat on the southeast corner and was the city's main black movie house. Erected in 1913, it was owned by Walter Kennedy, one of Knoxville's leading black citizens. While there were smaller theaters which catered to blacks, the Gem not only showed movies, but hosted stage shows as well.

On the northwest corner stood the Cal Johnson Building which housed the Economy Drugstore. Before Prohibition it had been home to one of the city's most popular saloons and was owned by Knoxville's most celebrated black entrepreneur. The upper floor contained the offices of black dentists, physicians, and lawyers.

Other businesses in the immediate area included restaurants, pool halls, shoeshine parlors, dry cleaners, sandwich shops, barbershops, beauty shops, fruit stands, and other small businesses. The area was, indeed, the heart and soul of the black business and social community.

Dr. Joseph Carthy, the white manager of the Economy Drugstore, noticed that as the evening of the riot progressed, usually genial blacks were expressing bitterness.

'Shortly after 11:00 o'clock," he said, 'I heard some shots on Central Avenue near Vine. This seemed to be the signal. At any rate Negroes, it seemed to me, poured down to the corner of Vine and Central from every direction. They came from the alleys and from the buildings. In a few minutes there were more than a hundred of them.

"A few white men were in the section and shooting soon began in earnest. As to who fired the first shots, the white men or black, I cannot say. It was then 11:36. I said to the boy helping me in the store that it was time we were getting out of the place.

'I had about $3,000 in the cash drawer and safe. I grabbed it and started my Ford and wheeled off up Vine toward Gay Street. Just before getting to Gay I heard and saw soldiers coming down Gay."

When county officials heard of the organized efforts of blacks and the reported sniping from their weapons, they sent two machine gun detachments to the area to contain their movement. Lieutenant James W. Payne, a regular army officer, volunteered to assist in the command of the guns.

One of his army buddies, Lieutenant James P. Cooper, said that Payne had no connection with the machine gun detachment that was sent from its post at the county jail. 'He was skilled in the handling of machine guns and he offered to go along to help direct the fire," said Cooper.

'One machine gun was mounted on each side of a little alley

on Vine Avenue about three hundred feet from Central. After assisting in mounting the guns, Lieutenant Payne walked up toward Central and approached within fifty feet of the avenue when a Negro stepped from behind the corner and began shooting in his direction.

"A sergeant, who was across the street, opened fire on the Negro with an automatic army pistol. Lieutenant Payne, in an effort to dodge the Negro's bullets, ran behind a telephone pole which placed him directly in the line of fire of his own men. About this time a crowd of civilians, seeing a number of Negroes coming up Vine toward Gay Street, shouted to the men manning the machine guns, 'Let them have it.' The two machine guns opened fire.

'The guns were sweeping a hail of bullets to both sides of the street and Lieutenant Payne fell from a dozen wounds in both legs and abdomen. He was nearly cut in half," said Lieutenant Cooper. He died before reaching the hospital.

Lieutenant Payne was attached to the Forty-sixth Infantry and was assigned to Camp John Sevier during the encampment of the Fourth Tennessee Infantry as a field instructor. He was considered an expert in the handling of machine guns and infantry equipment. His body was taken to his former home in Madisonville, Kentucky, escorted by a military detachment.

The next day, four blacks were wounded while attempting to resist search by soldiers. According to the *Journal and Tribune*,

> *At least three Negroes were more or less seriously injured by members of Company D on Depot Avenue near the Southern Railway Passenger Station between daylight and noon.*
>
> *The first of the three was wounded by a bayonet in the hands of Private E.J. Wafford of Company D. Private Wafford was*

> doing guard duty on the Gay Street Viaduct, he said, when a large Negro man approached. In accordance with orders from superiors, he says, he called to the man to halt. The man refused.
>
> As he neared the Negro, the latter hurriedly reached into his coat pocket for a revolver. But Wafford stabbed him with a bayonet. The Negro fell from the deep stab wound and was taken to a physician. Wafford says he took the pistol from the man.

Private R.T. Daniels also reported that he had shot a black man in the leg east of the Southern Station. The man had apparently been drinking and flashed a pistol in the presence of Daniels. When he ordered the man to drop the weapon, he said he was cursed and threatened by the man.

The third black was struck with a rifle butt by Private Clifford Lacy near the same spot. Lacy claimed that the man had tried to grab his sidearm. The fourth black man, Ben Glover, was shot in the thigh by a soldier near the corner of Magnolia and Central when he refused to halt and be searched. He was seriously wounded and taken to Knoxville General Hospital.

That same newspaper had a telling description of Hayes, who was interviewed by a reporter before being taken to Chattanooga for safekeeping:

> Hayes, talking through the bars, discussed the case freely declaring that he was not guilty and said that he had never seen this woman who was killed.
>
> At the time of the conversation with the reporter, Hayes was clad in a suit of solid pearl gray, black shoes and socks. The shoes had been half rubber-heeled, and the left had been half-soled. Hayes is the type of Negro usually referred to as 'yellow' among his race. He is considered 'handsome.'

## The Heat of a Red Summer

> *He is slender, almost frail, weighing one hundred twenty-nine pounds, and being five feet five inches tall. His countenance is that of an intelligent person.*

For several days after the riot, militiamen patrolled the streets of the city quelling disturbances. Black men were often stopped and searched for weapons.

For several weeks, an appeal was issued for those who took the weapons from break-ins to return them, no questions asked.

Maurice Hayes asked himself a thousand times, 'How can this be happening to me? I have tried to be fair and honest in all my dealings. I have not lived up to the letter of the law, but I have not tried to maliciously harm anybody." His reflections turned to his activities before his arrest.

# THE START OF A FATEFUL DAY

On Friday morning, August 29, 1919, Maurice Hayes decided to sleep late. He had spent much of the preceding Thursday night hanging out with friends until he met Sallie Jones near the corner of Vine and Central. After a few drinks and a sandwich, he took her to his house on Humes Street.

After they made love, he walked her to her room on Georgia Street about four blocks away. He returned home at 4:00 a.m. and decided to sleep until 10:00 a.m. There were two things he had to do later that day. It was a must that he see the exhibition baseball game, and he was committed to campaign for Mayor John McCulloch.

At 11:30 a.m., he headed for Brewers Park to see the first game of a doubleheader between the Knoxville Black Giants and the Chattanooga Black Lookouts. He had loved baseball from the time he was one of the stars on the Austin School team in 1903. He had kept up with the sport and personally knew many of the players in the Negro Southern League.

He was especially proud to claim as a friend John Claude "Steel Arm" Dickey who was born in Knoxville. His father, James Dickey, was the janitor at Mount Zion Baptist Church. The family lived on Willow Street not far from Hayes.

Dickey's fastball and control made him an excellent pitcher. He began his professional career with the Giants, but after two seasons he joined the Montgomery Grey Sox and was dubbed, "The Pride of the South." The team became league champions in 1921. His career was cut short when he was killed in a stabbing incident in Etowah, Tennessee, in 1923.

Hayes also knew Ralph "Pete" Cleague, who played with the Giants and later became an umpire in the Negro National League. He was also a friend of Larry "Iron Man" Brown who was second to none behind the plate.

Hayes's friends did not disappoint him as they went into action against the Lookouts that Friday afternoon. Although it was a hot, sunny day, the Giants cooled them with a 5-4 victory. After the game, Hayes went out on the field to shake hands and to congratulate them.

At 2:20, he left the ballpark and headed for the Jesse Rogers Livery Stable at 113 East Vine to rent a horse and buggy. His first stop was at the home of Mayor McCulloch in Whitfield Flats to pick up cards and campaign literature.

On the way back into downtown he stopped for his foster father, Will Hayes, at the corner of Vine and Central. The two men rode out Nelson Street to East Knoxville distributing materials into Park City and on through the tunnel to Love's Creek.

They stopped at the home of Mrs. Armstrong and at Mr. Whitson's place. Since Mr. Whitson was not at home, the Hayeses rode up to Mr. Whitson's workplace at the Southern Railway Shops. There, the men talked politics. Whitson, a white man, was asked to solicit the votes of the black men under his supervision to vote for Mayor McCulloch.

The Hayeses then stopped back at Mrs. Armstrong's house, picked up some watermelons, and headed down Washington

Pike for home. It was after 4:30 p.m. as the pair rode into Broad Street and turned into Morgan Street near Maurice's house.

Maurice took his father home, divided the melons with him, and went home to eat supper. He returned the horse and buggy to Wiley Rogers at the livery stable sometime near 8:00 p.m. After chatting with the men who worked there, he stood on the corner of Vine and Central talking to those who passed by and giving out poll tax receipts.

At 10:00 p.m., Maurice, on his way to Russell Lowe's house in Peed's Alley just off Broadway, stopped to talk with Deputy Sheriff John Kirk near the Catholic church at the top of Vine Street hill. The two men walked on to Kirk's house just a block or so from the church.

After turning south on Broad Street from Vine, Maurice stopped at the L&N Railroad Station and looked into the colored waiting room to see if anyone he knew was there. Seeing no one, he headed to Lowe's house which sat behind the station near Clinch Avenue.

Discovering that Lowe was not home, he went to the lunchroom/pool hall under the Clinch Avenue Viaduct. When told that Lowe was not there, he walked from Clinch to Gay Street, back down to Vine, and arrived on the corner of Vine and Central about 11:00 p.m. He again passed out poll tax receipts to those who had been registered to vote.

At Blaine McGhee's restaurant on Central he met cabdriver Jim Massengill. The two men went outside and got into Massengill's automobile to take a spin. They went north on Central to Jackson Avenue and turned onto Patton Street. They went west on Willow and back to Central and stopped at the Boston Café where Hayes made an unsuccessful effort to get the telephone number of Alice Brice.

Massengill dropped him off near the corner of Humes Street and Jackson Avenue near his home. He chose not to drive into Humes Street for fear the jagged rocks in the broken pavement would damage his tires. Hayes went to bed by 12:45.

He lived in a four-room house, which included a kitchen. He stayed in the front room and one room in the rear of the house was rented out to Daisy Williams and her husband who also had use of the kitchen. The room between them was rented occasionally to couples who wanted private time to themselves.

Barely asleep three hours, Hayes was awakened shortly after 4:00 a.m. Saturday morning by police officers banging on his door. "What do you want?" he said. They barged in and refused to respond to his question. When they asked why he had not opened the door sooner, he replied, "I am not in the habit of opening my door at this time of night unless I know who it is."

Hayes lay back on the bed as they began searching his room. They looked under the bed and went through the drawers while Hayes continued to ask what they were looking for. Finally, one of the officers, John Hatcher, asked what time he came home and if he had a revolver, a flashlight, and a pocketbook. Hayes responded, "I don't have any such things except a revolver in the dresser drawer."

Officer Tony Black examined the pistol, smelled it, and put it back in the drawer. He then asked Hayes if he had another pistol to which he replied, "No."

"It's a devil of a funny thing," Hayes said to the officers, "that you search through my house and won't tell me why. What do you want in here, Mr. Black?"

Black responded, "You'll find out soon enough." He then picked up Hayes's shoes and lightly scraped the bottoms.

Maurice's father, Will Hayes, who had showed the officers

where Maurice lived said, "What are you examining those shoes for, there ain't no mud on 'em."

Officer Black replied, "No, there's no mud on them, I'm just looking at the size of them. Get up and get your clothes on, Maurice."

"Am I under arrest?" said Maurice.

"Yes," said Black. "We are going to north Knoxville; hurry and put your clothes on. There has been a shooting out there and we want a woman to see you."

Officer Hatcher spoke up and said, "Yes, a woman has been killed."

Hayes said, "Lord 'o mercy! I done no killing; I've never been in that neighborhood before!"

When they arrived near the murder scene on Eighth Avenue, Officer Black brought Ora Smith, the cousin of the murdered woman, to look at Hayes. She walked up, pointed a finger and said, "He is the man," and quickly turned around and started away.

The astonished Hayes pleaded with Officer Black, "Mr. Black, please bring that lady back here and let her see better that I am not the man and have never been out here in my life." Black refused and put him in the patrol wagon and started back to town.

The ride back to town was a nightmare come true. How could he be identified as the murderer of a woman he did not know? How could he be accused of a crime in a house he had never visited? It had to be a horrible mistake. He cried on the shoulder of the elder Hayes as they neared the city jail.

After Maurice was placed in a cell away from the other prisoners, Officer Tony Black paid him a visit. "I got your yellow ass, now, boy," he said. "I told you you would have hell to pay. I have been after that cute ass of yours for a long time and I intend to see that you get what's coming to you.

"Nigger, what you need is a good ass whupping. You thought you were so high and mighty and so pretty. You thought Mayor McCulloch could save your ass from anything; well, you were wrong. I warned you about trying to act like white people—now you will be taught a real lesson."

All the while Officer Black spewed his blistering tirade on Hayes, he beat his billy club in the palm of his hand to further intimidate him. "I ought to beat your narrow ass right here and now boy—that's what I ought to do. But I don't have to dirty my hands with you. I'll wait until they get your pretty ass down in the state pen. They know how to handle smart niggers like you and they don't leave no scars. If there is enough of you left, maybe some of those gal boys might want it. I know one thing, nigger, you'll never touch another white woman."

"What have I done to you, Mr. Black; why do you hate me so much? You know I didn't kill that lady," said Hayes, on the verge of tears. He had heard Black's idle threats before, but now they weren't so idle. He actually began to fear for his life.

"I don't hate you," said Black. "I thought you were a good nigger until you started screwing around with white women. It didn't bother me so much that you sold liquor and ran a dice game in the back room of your place. I didn't even care about the nigger whores you were running, but you forget who you was— just a half-white nigger!

"Most of the niggers in this town know their place. Doctors, lawyers, teachers, bootleggers, and the rest. They know where they belong. But not you, boy. You just didn't know. Now you do because your ass is mine."

"But I never was disrespectful to you," responded Hayes. "I have tried to be a good citizen and I don't believe you have ever seen me in an awkward position with a white woman. In my business dealings and in my political activities, I have come in contact with a few white women, but that was on a business basis."

"Don't lie to me you little bastard! I know what you've been doing," said Black. "I just couldn't catch you in the act. One I know about is the redheaded gal who clerked at the Farragut Hotel. You met her during the times you delivered pints of liquor to guests staying there. She went to your house back in January. You know how I know? Lucille Washington told me. She was so mad at your ass, she could have killed you. Why she had the hots for you I don't know, but since you wouldn't give her the time of day, she told me about you and the redhead. Lucille was watching your house that night and saw you let her in. I only wish I could have caught you, you sorry son of a bitch. I would have rammed my nightstick up your yellow ass."

At that time one of the jailers came in and Black left the cell-block. Hayes was left severely shaken by the tirade and wondered what would happen next. Would some of the jailers do him harm? What were Officer Black's intentions?

Hayes was totally amazed that Black knew of his relationship with redheaded, big butt Molly McGregor. After all, they had only two meetings and they were done with the utmost secrecy. She would wait until dark and walk home from her house on Park Street, less than five blocks away, and go unnoticed. Both blacks and whites lived on Hayes's street.

What Hayes hadn't realized was that Lucille Washington, who told on him, was a maid at the Farragut Hotel and saw the unusual camaraderie between him and Molly. They did nothing openly, but if one watched the two of them carefully, the hanky-panky was almost obvious. The knowing smiles at each other and the passing of whispers could be the giveaway.

"How did I get involved with that woman?" Hayes asked himself. "She was no beauty and not much good in bed. The two times we were together were more than enough. There was no real excitement and we called it quits."

Lucille Washington, on the other hand, wanted a relationship with Hayes, but found him unreceptive. She was bold in her efforts to attract him, but he had no interest in her advances. He told her that he was seeing someone else and didn't want to be unfaithful. But Lucille knew better and awaited her opportunity to get even.

Maurice reflected on his dalliances with other white women, but couldn't see how these relationships had been such a big deal. He couldn't fathom that the small, tight-knit black community had noticed and fed the grapevine. He just never realized the danger in the whispers about his activities. His secrets were common knowledge.

## JUDGMENT IS RUSHED

As soon as Knox County Attorney General R.A. Mynatt heard the news of the murder and arrest, he consulted Judge T.A.R. Nelson and a special grand jury was ordered. At the insistence of Judge Nelson, the special session was held at the courthouse on Wednesday, September 3, 1919, at 9:00 a.m. It was the first time in memory that a grand jury in Knox County had been called in special session to investigate a case of any kind.

A similar procedure had taken place in neighboring Jefferson County just a few weeks prior. Judge Drinnon of that county held a quick trial of a black man accused of raping a white girl.

Less than a month after the Knox County grand jury indictment, the trial for Hayes began in criminal court on October 1, 1919. Governor Albert Roberts appointed former Knoxville Mayor Samuel G. Heiskell as special prosecutor to handle the state's case against Hayes.

The defense was handled by Reuben L. Cates, a former district attorney general. Two black lawyers, William F. Yardley and John W. Huff assisted the defense, but did not question witnesses. The trial ended in four days, on October 4, and Hayes was sentenced to die in the electric chair on November 28, 1919.

It had taken the jury less than twenty minutes to reach its guilty verdict. On January 20, after a round of appeals, the Tennessee Supreme Court reversed Hayes's conviction and ordered another trial. The second trial began on April 18, 1921.

In the second trial, Circuit Judge Xen Hicks sat by interchange for Judge T.A.R. Nelson. After the jury was called, selected, impaneled, and sworn, the indictment was read and the defendant offered a plea of not guilty.

Mrs. Ora Smith Parsons, the cousin of the slain woman, was called to testify for the prosecution.

Mr. Heiskell: "What kin, if any, are you to Mrs. Langley, the lady who was killed?"

"Her first cousin."

"Did you and Mrs. Langley sleep together?"

"Yes, sir."

"Now let's get to the night of the killing, you and Mrs. Langley slept together?"

"Yes, sir."

"Which side of the bed were you on?"

"I was on the side next to the wall."

"What was the first thing you became conscious of?"

"My cousin had me by the arm and was sitting up in the bed calling my name."

Mr. Heiskell questioned further: "When you woke up, what did you see?"

"I saw a Negro standing by the bed with a pistol in one hand and a flashlight in the other. The flashlight was in our faces."

"Now just tell the story from there on, Mrs. Ora, straight through in your own way."

"My cousin woke me up. She got on the other side of me. She stood up next to the wall and he commanded her to get down, that he was going to kill her and she laid down on the bed again and then she got up and he told her if she didn't lay down that he was going to shoot her. She laid down again and immediately got up and got down to the foot of the bed and looked out the window and then she got down onto the floor at the foot of the bed. He commanded her to get back into bed or he would kill her and she started as if she were going to the door and he told her if she didn't come back he was going to shoot her and he fired the shot."

"Who was the man that fired the shot?"

"Maurice Hayes."

"Is this Maurice Hayes here?"

"Yes, sir."

"Is that the man who fired the shot?"

"Yes, sir."

"Now, Miss Ora, when you woke up you saw him standing there with a flashlight in one hand and a pistol in the other?"

"Yes, sir."

"Did you say anything or did you speak?"

"The first I remember of speaking is when he threatened my life. I said, 'Save my life and take my money.'"

"And that was after the shooting took place?"

"Yes, sir."

"Now did this man standing there, that Nigger with the flashlight in one hand and the pistol in the other, put his hands on any part of you?"

"Yes, sir, my private part."

"Put his hand on your private part?"

"Yes, sir."

"Did he put his hand anywhere on Mrs. Langley?"

"Not that I know of."

"What did he say to you when he came back to the bed and put his hand on your person?"

"I don't care to repeat it."

"Now, Mrs. Parson, we don't want to embarrass you, but we would like very much for you to repeat what he said."

"I cannot do so."

"It was vulgar or bad talk anyway?"

"Yes, sir."

"Well, now, after he made the vulgar remark to you, how long did he stay there? Did he make any other remark after that?"

"Only he told me had a notion to kill me. I told him, 'Spare my life and take my money.' He then left."

Another witness for the prosecution was Knoxville Police Chief Ed M. Haynes.

Mr. Heiskell: "How long have you been chief of police?"

"Five years."

"How long have you been a policeman?"

"Thirty years."

"Did you occupy any other position in the city government?"

"Yes, I have been patrolman and sergeant, detective, chief of detectives, and chief of police."

Mr. Heiskell: "I will ask if you and several other officers went out to make an investigation or made any experiment in connection with the room in which Mrs. Langley was killed?"

"Yes, sir."

"Just in your own way and without question, describe to this jury what you did, the experiment you made, the appearance of the room, and when you went there with reference to the time of Mrs. Langley's death?"

Chief Haynes: "Well, I taken Mr. Fogarty out there, one of the city detectives, probably two or three or four days after she was killed, and we went out there about 7:30 or 8:00 o'clock at night and Mr. Dyer out there and his wife and probably another lady went into this room and first lit a lamp and set it on the table."

"Was Miss Ora Smith there?"

"Yes, sir, and Mrs. Langley's husband and we took the light out, blowed the light out and took a flashlight about the size that was claimed that this man used and flashed the light around in the room to see if we could see anybody in there and then we placed her in the bed the way she claimed she was in the bed and had the flashlight turned on her and then we turned it back over the wall back in the corner here—and there was no question about seeing anybody in the room with this flashlight—you could see very plainly in there. The wallpaper was white and the bed had a white spread on it and white pillowcases; that is about the experiment we made out there."

Mr. Heiskell: "In that room, could you tell a white man from a colored man?"

"Yes, sir."

"Could you tell a white man from a Mulatto man?"

"Yes, sir." "Tell the condition of the pistol when you saw it."

Chief Haynes: "Mr. Black gave me the pistol down at the city hall unloaded and I examined the pistol and it was a .38 hammerless Smith & Wesson pistol and there were four cartridges that looked like they had been in there for some time. They had a little dust around there where a man carrying cartridges in a revolver two or three weeks or a month, but one looked like it was a fresh shot and a new cartridge in the chamber and I turned it up and looked at it and it looked freshly fired."

One of the early defense witnesses was black patrolman Jim Smith, who drove the paddy wagon the night the officers went out to investigate the Langley murder scene. An eleven-year veteran of the police force, Smith was the son of Moses Smith, who was hired as the city's first black policeman in 1882.

The defense tried to establish the credibility of Jim Smith by referring to his father and attempting to name the high-powered citizens who had served as his father's pallbearers in 1887. But when asked if he remembered the names of any of those pallbearers, the prosecution objected and it was sustained.

Smith was then asked if he knew Maurice Hayes and Officer Tony Black. He answered in the affirmative to both questions. He also asserted that he and Black were on good personal terms with each other and often cooked and ate lunch together in the jail kitchen.

Mr. Cates: "Do you know Tony's feelings toward Maurice Hayes?"

"Yes, sir," Smith replied.

"Are they kind or unkind?" asked Cates.

"Unkind," was the response.

"What makes you think they are unkind?"

"Why, he has abused him around the jail there, cursed him to me. Maurice came up there one day and he sat down and he got after him and drove him away from there and told him that he thought he [Hayes] was cute and pretty, called him a son of a bitch and told him he ought to be in the penitentiary."

Mr. Cates: "Is that the only time you ever heard him abuse Maurice to his face?"

"Well, he talked a little rough to him that night this happened. He abused him that night. Just anytime me and Mr. Black—we worked there together and if we would go up

Jackson Avenue by his [Hayes's] place or get called up there, he would make some remark that he ought to be in the workhouse or the penitentiary."

Mr. Cates: "Were you given the opportunity to smell Hayes's pistol at his home when he was arrested?"

"I didn't want no opportunity there, but I said, 'As quick as I get to the jail, I will smell it.' At the city jail, when they came and brought Maurice, they smelled it again, and I smelled it."

On cross-examination by Mr. Houk, Mr. Smith was asked: "And after you saw them smelling the pistol, who was it you said to, 'Old Jim is going to smell that?'"

"I said that to myself. I seen them smelling it and looking like they were all dissatisfied about it, kept smelling it over and over."

"And you smelled no powder?"

"No sir, I did not."

"Are you sure of that? You can't be mistaken about that? Jim didn't smell no powder?"

"No, sir."

Mr. Houk: "Jim, you say that Tony Black was in the habit of cursing Maurice Hayes every time he saw him? What was it you said he called him at the city jail?"

Smith: "He would say something mean about him. He told him he thought he was pretty or cute or something, and that when he got through with him, he would be in the penitentiary."

Mr. Houk: "At any time prior to this homicide, did you hear Mr. Black express any opinion or say anything about Maurice Hayes?"

Smith: "He cursed him out one night at the city jail. He called him all kinds of little yellow bastards and he said he ought to be in the penitentiary, and he was a dirty Negro, and a whole lot about him."

"How many times have you heard Tony Black curse him?"

"Fifty or sixty times."

"Who else heard him curse Hayes down there?"

Smith: "They could not remember it if I was to tell you about it."

Houk: "You want this jury to understand your answer to that question to be that if you were to tell the names of anybody who had heard him curse him, they would not remember it now, is that it, that is what you stated?"

Smith: "The people who heard him abuse him are not being looked up. There is no use for me to tell you; they would not come down here and swear it."

Maurice was called to the stand and under questioning denied that he had ever met Mrs. Langley or Miss Smith. He said he had never been in their neighborhood before he was arrested and taken there for identification.

Mr. Cates: "What had you been doing the day of the night preceding the morning this woman was killed?"

"I had been in a horse and buggy engaged in scattering political literature for Mayor McCulloch."

"For Mr. John E. McCulloch, the mayor?"

"Yes, sir."

"Where were you that evening, Maurice?"

"That evening, my father and I were together with a horse and buggy and went out through East Knoxville to see some friends we knew. I got the horse and buggy at Jesse Rogers's stable on East Vine Avenue to drive around over the city amongst the colored voters that I knew in colored localities."

Mr. Cates: "Now, after you got the horse and buggy,

where did you find your father or was he with you when you got it?"

"I found my father on the corner of Vine and Central when I was starting out. I went to Mayor McCulloch's house and came back through town and met my father on the corner of Vine and Central and he hollered at me."

After all the testimony came to a close on April 22, 1921, the jury reported at precisely 9:11 a.m. with its guilty verdict.

Hayes took the verdict calmly. He held up his head and smiled. No shock reflected in his face. "I am innocent," he said. Defense attorney R.L. Cates immediately made a motion for a new trial.

The court had been called to order on that final day by Sheriff Cade at 9:00 a.m. They waited six minutes for the arrival of Mr. Cates, chief counsel for the defendant. The jury entered the room at 9:07. They walked in single file, proceeded to the judge's bench, and grouped around it.

"Gentlemen of the jury, have you reached your verdict?" asked Judge Hicks.

The answer was awaited in absolute silence by the packed courtroom. Not a soul moved. There was no coughing, clearing of throats, or other ordinary sounds to pierce the silence. The crowd hung on to every syllable as the pronouncement passed the lips of the foreman: "Guilty as charged, your honor!"

"Gentlemen, take your seats," said the judge, and the jurors moved to their seats in front of the bench. "Hold up your right hands," said Judge Hicks. "Is this the verdict of all of you?"

"It is," they responded.

"Gentlemen of the jury," said the judge, "you have my sympathy for the hard and long trial which you have sat through here. I appreciate your work. I thank you and discharge you."

"Sheriff, remand the prisoner," ordered the judge in his official tone.

As the deputies walked over to Hayes, defense attorney Cates said, "Don't worry, Maurice, be the same good prisoner you have been all along."

"Yes, sir," Hayes responded in a nearly inaudible voice.

He turned to his mother and kissed her and shook hands with two other black women who sat at the railing behind him. He held out his wrists to a deputy who put handcuffs on him and led him down the crowded aisle and out to West Hill Avenue and the county jail. He was placed in a cell with another black man.

This was another opportunity for Hayes to reflect on his nineteen months of a horrible nightmare come true.

He knew he was innocent and believed enough in the system to think his innocence would be figured out. He was well aware that he was a black man living in a racist society, but he thought that his lack of guilt was so obvious that his conviction would be overturned.

It still had not dawned on him that the crime for which he was to be punished was not the crime for which he was charged. No, he had not murdered anyone, but the crime he had committed was even worse in the eyes of white southern society. No, he had not even raped anyone, but his penalty was the same as a conviction for rape.

# The NAACP Takes an Interest

By now it had become obvious that the Hayes case was not about murder, but a case about racial injustice where the court would condemn a man innocent for one crime to punish him for violating one of society's taboos. While the charge and punishment were for murder, the real crime was having a black man bold enough to dally with white women.

A month after Hayes's first conviction, James G. Beck, a prominent and well-respected black man and organizer of the NAACP in Knoxville, on November 5, 1919, set in motion a spate of letters to the national office of the NAACP. Although the letter was not flattering to Hayes, it did get the organization's attention with hundreds of letters to follow.

In his letter to NAACP Secretary John R. Shillady in New York City, Beck wrote:

> *My Dear Sir: Mr. M.W. Dent, Secretary of the Chattanooga branch, was in our city today investigating the Maurice Hayes case. He came to my home and asked that I write the facts in this celebrated case. He was at a loss to know why the Chattanooga branch was asked to investigate said case when we had a branch here.*
> 
> *I explained to him that we had only recently received our*

*charter and was only too glad that he cooperate with us. He and I went over the facts very carefully together and are agreed that if it is at all possible that the National Association take some steps to help an innocent man.*

*Confidentially, I must say that the accused did not bear a wholesome reputation in the community; but we believe him innocent of the crime charged. If you can do anything, DO IT NOW! We think that a special detective could unravel the case very easily . . . please act with all possible haste.*

Secretary Shillady answered Beck's letter on November 21, 1919. Said he,

*In response to your letter of November 5 with regard to the Maurice Hayes case, I wish to say that while we are very sympathetic regarding it, it is absolutely impossible for us to advance any money. All our funds have been heavily tied up with expenses growing out of the Chicago riots and the defense of the Arkansas victims of injustices. Both of these cases involve a large number of cases of race discrimination.*

*We regret to be obliged to come to this decision, but, as a matter of fact, the funds of the Association are very limited, and our resources are small, and therefore, we are unable to go into many we should like to undertake.*

Another leader in the local NAACP, Reverend J.H. Henderson, pastor of Mount Zion Baptist Church, wrote a letter to NAACP National Secretary Walter White on April 30, 1921:

*. . . Our lawyers were at their best. There was no hurrying over things. Monday was used as you see selecting the jury, then*

the grind began and lasted until Thursday. All of Friday the battle royal raged until four p.m. when the case went to the jury. The closing arguments of Cates and Fowler are the talk of the town.

Our detective worked more than 20 days full time on the case. General Cates could not have done better for one who was kin to him. We accomplished two important things in the trial: We greatly weakened the state's case and we strengthened public sentiment in its belief that he is innocent. I might add, we got all of the killings that have taken place here before and since Hayes was confined into the record.

Mr. White, it is an awful thing. But we shall see that he shall not die. He shall have his freedom.

On July 17, 1921, Maurice himself wrote a letter to Major J.E. Spingarn of the national NAACP:

*My Dear Sir: Please permit me to appeal to you and beg of your kind consideration while in my most needful hour. You have no doubt learned of my poor circumstances. I am innocent and have been twice convicted in the lower courts for the crime of an uncaptured person.*

*I have been in prison since the race riot here nearly two years ago and now I am at the mercy of the public begging for assistance. My only hope is to raise money to meet the heavy expenses to appeal my case to the Supreme Court of Tennessee. Will you please consider and help me speak out on my behalf? I was falsely accused by prejudiced police officers who had previously threatened to imprison me.*

*Nearly $2,000 is yet needed to perfect my appeal to the high court where I beg for justice. Enclosed is one of my pictures that I offer the public and ask in return a contribution toward my defense.*

*Please help me if you can and God knows I will thank you with all my heart and soul. Please let me hear from you soon. My case will be decided in about two months. Please write to me direct here at the Knox County Jail.*

Hayes signed the letter, "Distressed Christian Friend, Maurice F. Hayes."

Reverend Henderson, in an earlier letter to the NAACP stated:

*It is a hard matter for us to get any information from police headquarters, as the [whole] push is against us. The county officials are our friends, but the city folks are fighting us all they can by suppressing valuable information from us.*

*In fact, Hayes is almost at the mercy of his old political enemies, both Whites and Negroes. This is their opportunity to put him out of the way. They are working it for all it is worth. I do not hear anything definite from his old enemies among Negro politicians, but I know, so far as helping him they are silent as lobsters.*

*They will tell you, however, that they do not believe he committed the crime, but they will go no further. Some of them are men of means but they won't give a dime in his defense. I cannot tell what they are doing under the cover.*

On August 1, 1921, Reverend Henderson wrote another letter to Secretary White thanking him:

*I wish to thank the Association for setting aside one hundred dollars for the case. I will need it to help pay our lawyers for their able service on the case. Everything is dull. We are not getting much money now.*

The Heat of a Red Summer • 53

* * *

Finally, on August 10, 1921, the national NAACP made its first news released on the Hayes case. Under the heading, NEW EVIDENCE TENDS TO SHOW MAURICE HAYES INNOCENT, the release stated the following:

*The National Association for the Advancement of Colored People, 70 Fifth Avenue, New York, today urged all possible aid in the defense of Maurice Hayes, twice convicted in Tennessee of the murder of Mrs. Bertha Langley in August 1919.*

*Since the arrest and conviction of Hayes, other white women have been attacked by a dark white man and the Knoxville, Tennessee,* Journal and Tribune *of August 3, 1921, prints the following cases: 'Mrs. Dan White, Hart Avenue. Man entered her home in September 1919 and told her if she screamed he would murder her as he had killed Bertha Langley. Mrs. Nettie Pingston, Maria Street. Home entered by man in autumn of 1919. He told her he would kill her as he had killed other white women if she screamed.'*

*The items tend to corroborate Hayes's assertion that he is innocent of the crime attributed to him. If the unknown criminal said he had killed Mrs. Langley as is quoted, every effort should be made to have that fact established legally, for the attack on Mrs. Dan White occurred after Maurice Hayes had been placed in prison charged with the murder of Mrs. Bertha Langley.*

*The Tennessee branches of the NAACP, with some aid from the National Office, have been fighting the case. The National Office feels that it is one meriting the assistance of such as can be given.*

And so from the first letter to the Association in November 1919 by James Beck to the last letter by Reverend J.H. Henderson in August 1921, it took the NAACP more than twenty-two months to respond positively to their requests. Was it too little, too late?

To answer those questions, it may be in order to examine the fiscal stance and the philosophy of the NAACP at that time. The organization had just celebrated its tenth anniversary in Cleveland, Ohio, June 21-29, 1919. Delegates to the convention were charged a fifty-cent fee. It entitled them to a badge and to attend the official programs and all meetings and entertainment.

The August 1919 *Crisis Magazine* reported of the conference:

> *We are a mighty organization. There in Cleveland, in the springtime of world peace, there met 265 delegates and members from 34 states of the Union, representing 75,000 members of the National Association for the Advancement of Colored People.*
>
> *This is a great weapon. How did they tell us to wield it in those 19 sessions with aggregate audiences of 10,000 persons?*

It then recounted the various lectures by noted individuals who had participated in the conference, giving detailed statements from the following:

> *Fight by Voting – Charles Edward Russell; Registered Fighters – Cora Finley; Fight the American Federation of Labor – E.K. Jones; The Sword of the Spirit – Oswald Garrison Villard; Southern White Allies – L.M. Favrot*

The article continued:

> *It was a mighty meeting. In many ways it was the greatest assembly ever held by Negroes in the United States. There have*

been larger assemblies among churches and fraternities, and meetings more intense, like the Niagara Movement at Harper's Ferry; but never so many Negroes from so many states met in earnest and continuous conferences.

Six of those in attendance came from Tennessee.
The September 1919 issues of *Crisis* reported:

*Thirty-six Negroes are known to have been lynched since the Armistice was signed last November—one of them a woman—six of the others lynched by being burned at the stake. Negroes are disenfranchised in whole or part in at least fourteen states of the Union.*

In an editorial of that same issue, Dr. W.E.B. DuBois said in part:

*We must not seek reform by violence. We must not seek vengeance. 'Vengeance is mine!' saith the Lord, or to put it otherwise, only infinite justice and knowledge can assign blame in this poor world, and we ourselves are sinful men, struggling desperately with our own crime of ignorance.*

*We must defend ourselves, our homes, our wives and children against the lawless without stint or hesitation; but we must carefully and scrupulously avoid on our own part bitter and unjustifiable aggression against anybody.*

*This line is difficult to draw. In the South, the police and public opinion back the mob, and the least resistance on the part of the innocent black victim is nearly always construed as a lawless attack on society and government. In the North, the police and public will dodge and falter, but in the end they will back right when the truth is made clear to them.*

\* \* \*

The October 1919 issue of *Crisis* quoted several items from newspapers across the country. One was picked up from a Knoxville newspaper:

> *August 30 - A mob stormed the jail at Knoxville, Tennessee, in search of Maurice F. Hayes, a Negro, who had been arrested on suspicion in connection with the murder of a white woman. The mob looted the jail, released prisoners, captured large quantities of confiscated whiskey and raged through the streets of the city. Race rioting developed.*

The February 1920 *Crisis* reports that:

> *According to our records, seventy-seven Negroes were lynched during the year 1919, of whom one was a colored woman, and eleven were soldiers; four white persons and three Mexicans were also lynched, a total of eighty-four lynchings.*

It listed the following according to states:

| | |
|---|---|
| Georgia | 22 |
| Mississippi | 12 |
| Alabama | 8 |
| Louisiana | 8 |
| Texas | 5 |
| Florida | 5 |
| North Carolina | 4 |
| South Carolina | 2 |
| Missouri | 2 |
| Colorado | 2 |
| West Virginia | 2 |

| | |
|---|---|
| Nebraska | 1 |
| Washington | 1 |
| Tennessee | 1 |
| Kansas | 1 |

The alleged crimes were:

| | |
|---|---|
| Murder | 28 |
| Rape and attempted rape | 19 |
| Trivial causes | 9 |
| Shooting and assault to murder | 7 |
| Insulting women | 7 |
| Intimacy with women | 4 |
| Bandits | 3 |
| Unknown | 2 |
| Burglary | 2 |
| Labor trouble | |
| Insurrection and quarrels | 2 |

The methods of punishment:

| | |
|---|---|
| Hanging | 43 |
| Shooting | 23 |
| Burning | 14 |
| Drowning | 2 |
| Cutting | 1 |

Between 1885 and 1919, 3,052 Negroes were lynched.

The March 1920 *Crisis* highlighted NAACP income and its budget. It reported a membership of 91,000 and the contributions it had received:

| Contributions of: | General Fund: | Special Fund: |
|---|---|---|
| $1,000 and over | 1 | 5 |
| 500 to 999 | 3 | 1 |
| 100 to 499 | 24 | 39 |
| 25 to 99 | 6 | 2 105 |
| 10 to 24 | 118 | 190 |
| 2 to 9 | 1,031 | 323 |
| Less than $2.00 | 60,411 | 23 |

Budget expenses were:

| | |
|---|---|
| Administrative and Supervision | $ 8,000 |
| Field Organization, Investigation, Travel | 17,000 |
| Dept. of Branches and Branch Bulletin | 3,000 |
| Education and Publicity | 11,600 |
| Office Expense (rent, clerks, postage) | 18,000 |
| Fight Against Lynching | 10,000 |
| Legal Defense | 10,000 |
| Total Expenditures | $78,000 |

The share of funds from most of the local branches was relatively small. They ranged from $2,000 from New York City to $25 from Adrian, Michigan. Knoxville sent $125.

It is obvious that the national NAACP faced tremendous burdens during its infancy and could not begin to assist in every worthy case. Perhaps the greatest revelation in the NAACP correspondence is the fact that men of means in Knoxville's black community decided not to participate in Maurice Hayes's defense.

One can only speculate as to why they adopted such a

stance. Were they afraid of reprisals if it became known they made contributions? Were they envious and jealous of the lifestyle Hayes led? Were they envious of the obvious influence he had in local politics? Or were they just so fed up with some of his illegitimate activities they did not care about his fate? Could it be that they thought he was getting what he deserved for fooling with white women?

Perhaps those men of means considered all of the above and wanted to get rid of an "uppity nigger" who was a stain on the community. It may help to introduce some of those leading people of the black community in 1919.

# SOME LEADING BLACK CITIZENS OF 1919

Knoxville's black society of 1919 was an interesting one. Hampered as a group by the laws of racial segregation, it was stifled. Saddled with the classless society it had to endure from within the community, it was frustrated. Oftentimes there was divided leadership or no leadership. Too often leaders sniped at each other and left the masses either confused or amused. Some of this may account for the lack of support in the Hayes case.

In general, the black community was either ignored or tolerated by the white population. Yet, so many whites depended on the services of black people. Most blacks in 1919 were employed in domestic services in white-owned homes. They were cooks, laborers, porters, janitors, and launderers. Most of the city's hotels were staffed by black bellmen and blacks drove many of the delivery wagons around town.

Stories in the local newspapers about blacks were few. Those which did appear were about lynchings in other places or about an "aged Negress" who had died. It was as though blacks were nonexistent in the scheme of everyday life. Almost no mention was made of their contributions to society, but it seems that a great effort was made to bid them farewell once they had died.

In a total population of 96,000 there were 11,000 blacks. Interestingly, there were sixteen black physicians, four dentists, and four lawyers. Blacks owned thirteen boardinghouses, twenty eating establishments, nine shoe repair shops, fourteen grocery stores, eight cleaning and pressing shops, all four shoe shine parlors, and both herb stores. At least one-fourth of the city's barbers were black.

After 1912, city political districts were so gerrymandered that it was impossible for any blacks to be elected to office. The same can be said for county offices. Obviously, there were "white jobs" and "colored jobs," which prohibited promotions for blacks. It was out of the question for blacks to participate in white social circles. All white service clubs were closed to blacks.

In public, black college professors, physicians, bellhops, and janitors socialized on the same level. While the college professors and physicians had more education, the bellhops made just as much money, and sometimes more. Since there were no real private clubs in the black community, everyone could go where his dollar took him.

The Masons, the Elks, the Odd Fellows, Knights of Pythias, and other lodges did not require economic consideration or education credentials for membership. They were largely concerned with a person's character and dedication to community service. It is amazing that these groups accomplished so much with such diverse memberships.

Knoxville's black physicians were in practice largely because of the Knoxville College Hospital. They could not practice at the Knoxville General Hospital so the college provided a much-needed facility. While a few of them made a decent living, there were too many for such a small black population. Yet, they all practiced medicine for more than twenty years.

There were at least thirty black churches, including Mount Zion Baptist, whose pastor, Reverend J.H. Henderson, led the effort to raise funds for Hayes. He was just one of four ministers who had a stable tenure during that period. The others were: Reverend James A. Pickett of East Vine Avenue Methodist; Reverend S.A. Downer, Shiloh Presbyterian; and Reverend E.M. Seymour of Rogers Memorial Baptist.

Perhaps the most important black leader of 1919 was the principal of Knoxville Colored High School, Charles Warner Cansler, who had been principal of the high school since 1911. He had read law and was admitted to the Knoxville bar in 1892. He unsuccessfully run for the state legislature in 1894. Cansler was organizer of the group that established the Colored Library in 1917. He became a schoolteacher in 1900.

James G. Beck, previously mentioned, was secretary of the local NAACP. He was a 1906 graduate of Knoxville College and went to work in the post office in 1913 as the first black postal clerk in the state of Tennessee. He and his wife established the Colored Orphanage in 1919.

Highly respected as a member of the intelligentsia, Beck also was a local baseball celebrity, having excelled in that sport as a student at Knoxville College. He and his wife, Ethel, were quite successful in their real estate ventures.

Of course, Reverend J.H. Henderson, who had come to Knoxville in 1917 from Hot Springs, Arkansas, was at the forefront of the movement to save Hayes. At his church he organized efforts, paid off all debts there, organized a band and orchestra, initiated a church bulletin, and acquired more property for expansion in order to build a community house and apartment building.

Another influential person was Webster L. Porter who edited The East Tennessee News. Porter was either loved or hated by those who really knew him. His newspaper constantly railed against one community leader or another.

He constantly rode the back of Cansler because Cansler did not have a college degree. Porter accused him of living off the taxpayer all his adult life. He accused the Becks of scheming and getting rich off the poor. His newspaper was full of derogatory stories about them.

Porter's match in hurling stones was Dr. James H. Presnell, who was known as the city's "bronze mayor." In a signed letter he said Porter was known in the community as the "goat man," and the "man once accused of rape." He further described a girl running from Porter's office screaming with her "face scratched and clothes torn from her back." He further accused him of being a wife beater and other things.

Eventually, even Reverend Henderson ran into some difficulties. During a controversy at his church, the church split and he returned to Hot Springs, Arkansas.

So, indeed, the name calling, backbiting, and strife within the black community could not promote a healthy front to raise money for Maurice Hayes.

# The Slam of the Big Steel Door

Hayes had been arrested early Sunday morning on August 31, 1919. During and between his trials he spent twenty months in prison. While his stay at the Knox County Jail was no tea party, his friends came to see him. His foster mother brought him some of his favorite foods, and the black community understood his plight and offered moral support.

In the state prison at Nashville, he also had sympathetic supporters. Several preachers visited him on a regular basis and gave words of encouragement. Yet, prison life there was a living hell.

All the while, Hayes professed his innocence. He knew that his first trial had been little more than a kangaroo court to satisfy the thirst of those clamoring for vengeance. The evidence against him was less than circumstantial, but the jury made its decision in less than twenty minutes.

His hopes for justice brightened when the Tennessee Supreme Court ruled that he had not gotten a fair trial and ordered a new one. But the second trial was just as cut-and-dried as the first. It lasted five days and again the verdict was guilty.

This swift justice in the courts may be the reason for the lack of lynchings in Knoxville. Mobs didn't think it necessary to have a necktie party when they knew the judge and jury would see things their way. And the local newspapers did their part to help convict the accused with their graphic vitriolic descriptions of the crimes.

The newspapers also portrayed the accused as fiends who were no more than animals on the prowl. In their zeal to describe these, however, they inadvertently showed some of the accused people to be retarded and unable to adequately defend themselves in a court of law.

Several cases of this type are detailed in Knoxville newspapers of the late 1800s. One curious aspect was the keen interest in getting the accused to confess to the crime after he had been convicted. There was great disappointment when one went to the gallows claiming his innocence.

The November 22, 1890, *Knoxville Journal* described in minute detail the official execution of Jackson Staples, who was hanged at the Knox County Jail the day before. Said the *Journal*:

> *Yesterday morning about nine when the reporter first saw Staples, he had not changed at all and his face was lit up with that same sickly grin it has worn doubtless from birth. In response to a remark concerning the short time he had to live, Jackson reiterated his innocence and said that he was all the more ready for the end to come.*
>
> *At 10:50 Staples offering no objection, the front door of the jail was thrown open to the crowd of men and women, mostly Negroes who had occupied the street in front of the building since about nine o'clock. They were allowed to pass through the lower floor of the jail to see and shake hands with the man who had but a short time to live.*
>
> *Staples was dressed in his best suit of clothes and he looked*

fine. They fit him 'shust like de baber on de wall.' His shoes had been finely polished, a clean shirt, collar and necktie had been given him and in fact he never looked better in his life.

As soon as the crowd had been hustled out of the jail, Staples was told that two clergymen were waiting to see him. The two Colored gentlemen read passage after passage of the Bible appropriate to the occasion, interspersing them with hymns.

'I have no confession to make,' said Jackson. 'I am an innocent man, have accepted Christ, and feel positive I shall meet him in heaven above.' It was alarming to the gentlemen. If he was innocent of the crime, what a terrible mistake to hang him, if guilty why would he refuse to confess?

At 11:40 the coffin arrived from undertaker Jarnigan's rooms. It was encased in a large wooden box, which was carried into the jail. Then the coffin was lifted out. It was a plain imitation rosewood one, nicely lined and ornamented on the exterior.

Attorney T.A.R. Nelson, who by the way, was not Staples's lawyer called to see the prisoner. The attorney also tried to get a confession from him, but was unsuccessful in the attempt. Staples merely said that he was innocent and would die with assurance that he would be saved. He knew he had been wrongly suspected of the crime, but since the laws of the land under these circumstances condemned him to die, he was entirely ready.

At 2:40 Staples walked to the gallows. His hands were cuffed behind him, his legs were tied together, and a black hood was placed over his head. In two minutes the lever was pulled and he fell through the trap.

Unfortunately, it had not been properly set and Staples died not of a broken neck, but of strangulation. For twenty agonizing minutes doctors examined the body before finally pronouncing him dead. Although some 1,500 people had gathered to witness the event, the sheriff had decided to allow no spectators.

Obviously, Staples suffered from some kind of retardation, but that didn't matter to the court. He was accused of a heinous crime and had to pay for it. Other documented trials in Knox County also indicate that some of the men hanged were mentally challenged.

Perhaps when the mob in 1919 rushed the jail to lynch Maurice Hayes, it was not sure the judge and jury would find him guilty. After all, he was a "different kind of Negro." He had influence in high places and people wondered how much effort his biological father would exert on his behalf. They wondered if the necktie party was the only sure way to make him pay.

Now convicted with all appeals exhausted, Hayes began his last days behind the walls of the stark, cold state prison in Nashville with little hope except for the pleas to newly elected Governor Alfred A. Taylor to spare his life.

Taylor, who would be the pivotal figure in the life or death of Maurice Hayes, was elected governor in 1921 and the oldest person to occupy the executive chair. The seventy-three-year-old diehard won his election against incumbent Albert H. Roberts by more than 40,000 votes. No stranger to state politics, he had run against his brother, Robert Love Taylor, for governor of Tennessee in 1886.

In that race, called the War of the Roses, the Democrats wore white roses in support of Robert, and Alfred's backers wore red roses. The two brothers hit the campaign trail playing fiddles.

Although they entertained the crowds, they also discussed the serious issues of the day.

After the votes were counted, Robert had beaten his brother but there was no bitterness between them.

Alfred Taylor was born on August 6, 1884, in Carter County in east Tennessee. His father, Nathaniel Taylor, was an 1840 graduate of Princeton and a political figure in his own right. He served in the U.S. Congress from March 30, 1854 to March 3, 1855, but was defeated for reelection. He moved his family to New Jersey and was President Andrew Johnson's commissioner of Indian affairs from March 26, 1867 to April 21, 1869.

Young Alfred attended Duffield Academy in Elizabethton, Tennessee, and the schools of Edge Hill and Pennington Seminary in New Jersey. He studied law, was admitted to the bar in 1874, and set up his practice in Jonesboro, Tennessee.

He was a member of the state House of Representatives from 1875 to 1877. He served in the U.S. Congress from March 4, 1889 to March 3, 1895. He chose not to run for reelection and settled down to practice law in Johnson City, Tennessee, and often lectured on agricultural issues.

As Tennesseans apparently grew tired of the Democratic rule of the two previous governors, they turned to Taylor to run for governor as a Republican. Along with his family providing string music to back up his speeches, he offered winning wit and knowledge on issues of the day to win the election. He was inaugurated on January 15, 1921.

In March 1922, with all appeals exhausted, groups and individuals familiar with the Hayes case began writing Governor Taylor on Hayes's behalf. Supreme Court judges Colin P. McKinney and Nathan L. Bachman wrote the following letter:

* * *

*Dear Sir: I have been asked to request you to stay execution in the case of Maurice Hayes. Upon the record in that case, I was and am now convinced the evidence fully warranted the sentence imposed. However, I am advised that a number of affidavits have been presented to you (some of which it was sought to have the Court consider, but which were excluded because legally incompetent), as well as other facts and circumstances relating to the question of identification.*

*If this matter is sufficient to raise serious doubt in your mind as to Hayes's guilt, then it would, in my opinion, be eminently proper to grant a respite in order that the question might have further investigation. Not knowing the weight of the additional matter, I am not in a position to advise you, but feel no harm could come from a responsible delay in order that the same might have a full investigation.*

On March 14, 1922, Governor Taylor rendered his response:

*The pardoning power as it relates to capital cases, especially, has been placed in the hands of the governor not, as I conceive it to be used according to his own inclination, sympathies, likes and dislikes, but to be exercised only to correct any mistakes shown to have been made.*

*The friends of Maurice Hayes have asked me to commute his sentence to life imprisonment on the ground that it would soon develop who the marauder is or was who killed Mrs. Bertha Langley. Yielding to these numerous requests I gave him a respite of ninety days, but nothing so far of a substantial nature has been brought forward showing that some other than Maurice Hayes perpetrated the crime.*

Numerous theories have been advanced. The responsibility for the fate of Maurice Hayes rests with the courts and juries of Tennessee and not upon me.

Hayes's counsel, J.A. Fowler, made a final appeal to the governor without result.

Hayes, sensing that all appeals would fail, wrote the following letter to one of Knoxville's black weeklies, *The East Tennessee News*:

> I beg to drop a line to the public through the columns of your kind paper and to thank the justice loving citizens for their undivided interest in defense of my innocence.
>
> The writer of these lines is an innocent man who is being forced to sacrifice the blood of innocence upon the altar of prejudice. I am innocent before God and man, but innocence makes no difference to Uncle Alf Taylor, Tennessee's fox hunting governor, even if he is lawfully empowered to save the life of innocent men.
>
> I was a businessman with money. I have been sent to my death without proof or motive for conviction and he is the first governor Tennessee has ever had that denies his lawful power to act, as he says although he recently did for one condemned man the same thing that I begged him to do for me.
>
> I was an officer of the law under a democratic administration and incurred the enmity of some republican politicians who have dug my grave. I was at least known to be honest by the best elements of Knoxville's citizens, which element firmly believes in my innocence and will not hesitate to tell 'Old Limber' that he is deliberately murdering me in cold blood while the Knoxville police make fun of his ability as governor.
>
> After the governor read the record in my case he openly

*expressed to both white and colored witnesses his firm belief in my innocence and advised my dear old parents and friends that they need not fear as to my future, regardless of the conviction by two prejudiced juries. But since that time politics have begun to boss the job and, I am reliably informed that the Commissioner of Insurance advised the governor that if Maurice Hayes (even if he is innocent) should be allowed to live, it would cost him 50,000 votes in his race for reelection.*

*If I am allowed to live it would cost him 50,000 votes in his race for reelection and right and justice gave way to politics and robbed me of my life. I begged the governor with an innocent heart not to allow the cause of justice to miscarry and an innocent life be taken, but he heeded not my plea, nor the thousands of respected white citizens of Knoxville.*

*Instead he allows my life to be taken and deliberately stains his hands with innocent blood. With my dying breath, I appeal to the Negro voters of Tennessee to vindicate my death by aiding forever removing from political life this fox hunting governor who with 'Ole Limber' is chasing the Negro Republicans to seek protection under a future Democratic administration.*

*He knows his court is a court of clemency and a court of last resort. His word was the law, yet he recklessly forces me to die unjustly, with a firm belief in his own heart of my innocence. If that loving Democrat 'Bob' Taylor, could rise up in his grave, he would point the finger of scorn and shame in the face of his Republican brother and call him a cold blooded murderer.*

*But I die and go to God and I leave this earth with my innocence buried in the hearts of thousands of white citizens of Knoxville and Knox County, and through the state. Goodbye.*

\* \* \*

Just a few weeks before, on February 27, Hayes had written a letter to Mrs. Ora Smith Parsons, the cousin of murdered Bertha Langley, to ask that she reconsider her testimony in identifying him as the killer:

*Dear Mrs. Parsons: I humbly beg to write you just a word in a plea for your kind consideration, while I sit on the brink of the grave, burdened down in a death cell awaiting the death signal that will send my innocent life into eternity and force me to bid goodbye to this world, upon the strength of your word.*

*The Lord guides me to write you and may his tender mercies touch your heart for justice's sake, while I humbly kneel with tearful eyes begging for just the least consideration from you, whose mistaken words have forced me into the very shadow of an unjust death, and in a few days hence, in going to my death I am forced to give up my life upon a mistake of your word alone.*

*My life, all I have in this world, is to be taken from me solely upon your word alone. God knows, and I know that I am entirely innocent of the murder of Mrs. Langley. I truly regret her death, as I would any person's. I was never at the house in which you and Mrs. Langley lived or on the street which it stood, and I knew nothing whatever about the crime until I was told about it after my arrest.*

*Mrs. Parsons, please, I beg to recall your memory a mistake of just a few months ago in Knoxville. Frank Martin, colored, was mistakenly accused by a young white lady who said Martin attacked her and fought her face-to-face for over twenty minutes in broad daylight on the railroad tracks. She was very much mistaken and her heart was touched by God who looked upon the mistake, and to relieve herself she corrected her serious mistake that might have meant death for an innocent man.*

*Mrs. Parsons, please consider. She made her mistake in broad daylight. You made your mistake in the nighttime, when it was much easier to be mistaken. For God's sake, won't you please consider your mistake that calls for the taking of my innocent life?*

*I am only mercifully pleading for fairness in defense of my innocence, and to you alone after such a serious and unjust place my life is in, while the unknown murderer of Mrs. Langley is still free and has probably shot and killed many others, the very same way, since I have suffered in prison for his crime. I cry out for your correction of your mistake that unjustly burdens my soul.*

*God above reads the secrets of all hearts. He sees us at all times and knows about our sins. He knows I am innocent. Would you not be sorrowful the rest of your days if I am put to death on your word alone? If I can only live, I'll spend the balance of my poor life behind prison walls paying a debt I do not owe, which is hard indeed, but death is dreadful, and so much harder and so unjust.*

*I plead for life instead of death. After I am dead it will then be too late, but God will teach, and may make your life miserable. He will bury it into your heart as long as you live, that I died innocent, upon your word alone. Please by your Christian mercy let me live to thank you and God for the right.*

Mrs. Parsons received the letter at the Standard Knitting Mills where she worked. After some prodding, she showed the letter to news reporters still interested in the case.

She told them she had responded to Hayes by messenger and said to him that her conscience was clear, and that she was not troubled with her responsibility in identifying him as the killer, and that she had not changed her opinion about who killed Mrs. Langley.

Languishing behind bars for 926 days had taken a visible toll on Hayes. His body had become wracked with physical pain and his mind began to play tricks as his hopes for a reprieve glowed and dimmed. But it was the lonely ten months in the state prison at Nashville which proved his undoing.

The heat of summer in that stark, cramped cell left his body dehydrated and his lungs suffering from the lack of cool, fresh air. He never got accustomed to the prison smells of moldy concrete, urine, and sweaty bodies. He could not accept the invasive forays of flies, roaches, and rats into his tiny cell.

The cold of winter destroyed his health. At one time he suffered a bout with pneumonia. Influenza attacked his body more than once and he constantly had a head cold.

All of these things affected his eating habits. Then, too, he never quite got used to prison food—none of the meat was ever fresh or identifiable—he almost never knew what he was eating. Once he found parts of a grasshopper in his vegetables.

As a result his small body began to deteriorate. Six months after his transfer to state prison, he weighed only 98 pounds. He had to be fitted with clothes from the state juvenile division where delinquent boys were incarcerated.

He was a constant patient in the prison infirmary, which provided little help for his condition. He began to have nightmares, which were all too real. Some nights his screams could be heard throughout death row.

While his overseers were sympathetic, he was still just another prisoner convicted of murder. They were never cruel to him, but he felt the cruelty of the system.

Hayes missed the joy of human contact. In his free life he

loved to mix and mingle and was gregarious with his friends and associates. Now, he was isolated and had only an occasional guard with whom to exchange pleasantries. His only salvation was his writing. He wrote letters and poems decrying the injustice done to him. He thanked his supporters. He blasted those who were responsible for his predicament. Sometimes his words just rambled.

In the end, Maurice Hayes was a mere shadow of the dashing figure he cut to make women want to be in his arms. The once- smooth golden skin was now pale and lacking. The handsome smile was now almost never seen. The precise agile steps had given way to a walking cane, and later, crutches because of an undiagnosed condition.

The fateful morning of March 15, 1922, arrived with a blustery wind. The windows of Hayes's small cell rattled with every gust. Although the temperature outside was relatively warm, the piercing wind through the cracks made it seem much cooler. Hayes sat on his bunk with a blanket wrapped about his shoulders.

At precisely 5:00 a.m., Prison Warden James Davis, the Reverend S.L. McDowell, and two guards unlocked Hayes's cell door and approached his bed. At first, the emaciated man did not hear them enter, but after catching a glimpse of them he shuddered and cried out, "Oh, Lord, please don't let them take me to my death! Lord, I have suffered so long and you know my heart. Please deliver my body from this ordeal."

Immediately Reverend McDowell rushed to his bedside and threw his arm around Hayes's shoulder, and tried to offer some comfort. "Calm yourself, my boy," he said. "The Lord won't let any of us shoulder more than we can bear. As we walk through the valley of the shadow of death, have no fear for the Lord is with us."

The two guards helped Hayes to his feet, each holding him under an arm as they slowly walked from the cell. The warden walked in front of them as Reverend McDowell walked in the rear, softly praying. Hayes was in silent tears as he painfully hobbled to his final destination. As he stumbled and almost fell, his father and Reverend McDowell grabbed him under each arm.

He seemed to have come to grips with his fate and showed no outward emotion. For almost three years he had pleaded his case in the courts. He had waged a letter-writing campaign claiming his innocence. His story was carried in various newspapers. He got the National Association for the Advancement of Colored People interested in his case. He had prayed and challenged the legal and political system, but to no avail.

Even as he was strapped into the electric chair he exhibited no overt reaction. As the hood was placed over his shaved head, he closed his eyes as if expecting to go to sleep. He made only a slight move to be more comfortable as the straps were tightened around his arms and legs.

The night before, he had been asked what he wanted for his final meal. He ordered sausage and scrambled eggs with grits, hot biscuits, and coffee. When the meal came, he took two sips of the coffee and left the rest untouched. He now weighed less than 90 pounds.

At 6:00 a.m., the lethal voltage ended the life of Maurice Franklin Hayes. There was only a slight twitch as the electricity passed through his frail body. The prison physician pronounced him dead at 6:10. The body was immediately taken to the Taylor Undertaking Parlor for preparation to be transported to Knoxville.

Along with Reverend McDowell and other prison officials

who witnessed the execution was Will Hayes, who had traveled to Nashville to claim his son's body. Although the elder Hayes was only fifty-eight years old, he appeared to be much older. His years of working in the vinegar factory and his agonizing over the fate of Maurice had ruined his health.

Mr. Hayes rode to the railroad station in the horse-drawn hearse from the Taylor Undertaking Parlor with the casket bearing his son. As the casket was loaded into the baggage car, he thanked Mr. Taylor and Reverend McDowell for all of their kind gestures and climbed into the colored passenger car for the long, agonizing trip home.

For once Hayes could be alone in his thoughts and reflect on the joys Maurice had brought him. He thought of the times he took the young lad to Brewer's park for ball games and church picnics. He recalled taking him to his first horse race at Cal Johnson's racetrack in Burlington when Maurice was only six years old.

He remembered when Maurice caught his first catfish on the bank of the Tennessee River near First Creek—how proud he was of that fish! Hayes also recalled how good a student Maurice was in school and gloried in his athletic ability. He was proud to call Maurice his son.

Of course, there were those early days when he was not so sure. He wondered if Maurice's background would bring unhappiness to him and his wife. He wondered what Maurice's friends would say to him as he got older. He was bothered by what his own friends might say in the heat of anger or vindictiveness.

Hayes Sr.'s wife, Hazel, worked in the home of one of Knoxville's wealthiest white families, the McFarlands, who were distant kin to John McCulloch, the biological father of Maurice. Mr. McFarland told Hazel of this fine young baby that needed a good home. He explained that the mother was a young colored woman who had been dating a white man. Since Mrs. Hayes and her husband could not have children of their own, McFarland asked her to talk to her husband about adopting it.

After much discussion the couple thought favorably of the idea. They had good Christian hearts, knew the baby needed a home, and they surely wanted to be parents. They told McFarland they were ready to adopt.

The day they met Sara Lou Smith, who came to give them her son, they made the connection with Maurice's heritage. They had heard the whispers about her and John McCulloch. They were also aware of the kinship between the McFarlands and the McCullochs. But all of that made no difference; they were gaining a beautiful son.

As the years went by, no one ever acknowledged that John McCulloch was the father of Maurice, but it was kind of understood. Hazel Hayes often received extra money from her employer to help with household expenses. As Maurice grew older, McCulloch paid him to do chores and to run errands; he seemed to be proud of his offspring.

In the scheme of things, the secret was really no secret. White men had always fathered children with black women. It was a common occurrence during slavery, and 1887, the year Maurice was born, was barely twelve years after slavery had been abolished. So, the secret meant not to discuss it openly.

For thirty-four years Will Hayes had the fulfillment of a good, productive son. It was what he and his wife desired. Now, on the long, lonely train ride to Knoxville there was only emptiness. The joy of his life lay in a box in the car ahead of him. He could only imagine the heartache of his wife awaiting their arrival.

# His Testimony in Court is Recalled

During the heartbreaking ride, the older Hayes reflected on the last trial of his son Maurice and recalled the testimony he had given on that fateful day, April 18, 1921. Could he have answered the questions in a better way to have made a difference? Could he have remembered more details that would have helped to save his son's life?

He recalled the questions asked by Attorney Cates, Maurice's chief defense counsel:

Q – Uncle William, you are Maurice Hayes's father?

A – Supposed to be.

Q – How old are you?

A – I will be fifty-seven years old the sixth of January coming.

Q – How long have you lived in Knoxville?

A – I have been living here upwards of fifty-odd years.

Q – For who did you work last in the city?

A – The last I worked for Maurice in his business here.

Q – Did you ever work for Mr. Spiro?

A – Yes, sir. I worked for him over thirty-five years.

Q – And why did you quit working for him?

A – Well, the doctors advised me to quit.

Q – On account of health?

A – Yes, sir. The vinegar was too strong for my lungs and they advised me to quit.

Q – Mr. Spiro was in the vinegar and cider business?

A – Yes, sir.

Q – Do you remember the fact of Maurice being arrested on this charge?

A – Yes, sir.

Q – One night in August, 1919?

A – Yes, sir.

Q – And the fact that the officers came to your house that night?

A – Yes, sir.

Q – Did you go down to Maurice's place when the officers came?

A – No, I followed them down there.

Q – Were the officers in the room when you got there?

A – Yes, sir.

Q – Did you hear Maurice or the officers say anything about opening the door?

A – I hear Maurice asked or answered and say, 'Open the door, Maurice, it is the officers" something similar to that and he got right up and opened the door.

Q – Were you in the room with the officers?

A – Yes, sir.

Q – Did you see Mr. Black do anything about Maurice's shoes?

A – I seen him when he had the shoe up scraping it with his thumbnail like.

Q – What did you ask him?

A – I said, 'Why, there is no mud on his shoes, what are you scraping it for"and he said, 'Why I am trying to see the size or the number, trying to make out the size or number"I think it was the number. I am not positive.

Q – Did you see anybody do anything with a pistol there that night?

A – I saw them with it. They asked Maurice whereabouts was his gun and he said it was in the drawer and they pulled out the drawer and broke the pistol down and each one smelled it and they held it to my nose and asked me to smell it and I smelled it and they asked me if I smelled powder and I said, 'No, I smell no powder."

Q – Did you smell powder?

A – No, sir.

Q – Was there a smell of powder about it?

A – No, sir.

Q – Did it have the appearance of having been recently fired?

A – No, sir, just an old cold pistol.

Q – What did they do with the pistol then?

A – Now, a little bit after that they put it back in the drawer and then afterwards they got it out again.

Q – Did they make a search there for other pistols?

A – They asked, 'Whereabouts is your other pistol, Maurice?" and he said he had no other one and they asked for a flashlight and he said he had loaned it to Deputy Sheriff King five or six months ago and he never had brought it back.

Hayes was then cross-examined by Prosecutor Houk:

Q – You testified in the other trial of this case, didn't you?

A – I suppose so.

Q – Did you or not?
A – Yes, sir, I did.
Q – You were the last witness put on the stand?
A – Probably I might have been.
Q – Don't you remember that you were the last witness put on the witness stand and heard all the testimony in the lawsuit?
A – Before?
Q – Yes.
A – No, I never heard none of it.
Q – You were out under the rule before?
A – Yes, sir.
Q – Now you say that the first you knew about this matter was when the officers came to your house?
A – Yes, hunting Maurice.
Q – Did they come to your house first?
A – Yes, I suppose so.
Q – Now, Uncle William, you testified before that you told all you knew about it?
A – No, sir.
Q – What didn't you tell before that you have told this time?
A – I didn't have time ~~I was~~ not asked ~~I was~~ dismissed very suddenly.
Q – What didn't you tell before that you have told this time?
A – I don't know.
Q – Did you testify before anything about Andy Black picking up the shoe and scraping the bottom of that and saying he was looking for a number?
A – I don't know ~~I was~~ not asked that.

Q – You didn't testify that before?
A – No, because I was not asked that.
Q – Did you testify that before Maurice told the officers in your presence that he had loaned his flashlight to Ethel King?
A – Perhaps I did, I don't know.
Q – You think you did?
A – Yes, sir.
Q – That is your best recollection?
A – Yes, sir.
Q – Now you say you looked at that pistol?
A – I saw it in their hands, yes, sir.
Q – You say you smelled the barrel of it?
A – Yes, I smelled the pistol when they broke it down.
Q – You didn't examine the cartridges?
A – No.
Q – You never examined the cylinder or chambers that held the cartridges?
A – I think they took the cartridges out of it and then they put them back in the pistol.
Q – You never examined it?
A – No, sir, they never gave it to me.
Q – When you got down there, where were the officers?
A – It seems to me they were at the next house on the porch, some of them, and some of them were in the yard.
Q – What did they do after you got there in an effort to wake Maurice up or get him to answer the door?
A – Well, they came over to Maurice's and they called Maurice and they knocked.
Q – How many times did they knock?

A – I don't know, but a few times.
Q – Well, was the knocking loud or soft?
A – Well, medium I suppose.
Q – What was he knocking with?
A – I think it was a stick.
Q – A policeman's billy?
A – I don't know, it was a stick.
Q – You know a policeman's billy?
A – I suppose it was. I don't know what it is I suppose it was.
Q – What makes you suppose it?
A – Well, I don't know that they had anything else.
Q – Were you right there with them?
A – Yes.
Q – And yet you don't know what they were knocking with?
A – No, I don't know whether it was a police billy or what.
Q – You could tell it was something hard?
A – Yes, sir.
Q – He struck the door?
A – Yes, sir.
Q – How many times did they strike the door?
A – Maybe three or four or maybe more, I don't know.
Q – What else did they do while you were there in an effort to get Maurice to answer after they came back from the other house?
A – I think they went to the window and one of them or maybe two, and they came back and said, 'He is in there" and knocked and Maurice answered.
Q – How many times did they call Maurice before he answered?

A – Two or three or four or maybe not so many.
Q – How many times did you call him?
A – I don't think I called him airy time.
Q – Where were you when he answered the door?
A – Right on the porch with the officers, I may have been at the edge of the porch, but I was right there.
Q – Near the front door?
A – Yes, sir.
Q – Just as soon as they knocked on that door Maurice got up?
A – As soon as he answered he got up.
Q – What did he say when he answered?
A – 'Ho-ho" that way, and they said, 'Open the door" and I think they said, 'It is the officers" and he opened it.
Q – You saw them turn the flashlight into the window.
A – I didn't see that.
Q – You saw them at the window?
A – They were passing backwards and forwards I don't know whether they throwed it in the window or not.
Q – There was a flashlight there?
A – Yes, sir.
Q – You don't remember about that?
A – Yes, I think they had a flashlight.

Hayes then answered redirect questions about Mr. Cates:

Q – Uncle William, did you notice whether his trousers were damp?
A – No, sir, or nobody else. His trousers were hanging on the bed and nobody touched his trousers the legs were hanging off the bed at the edge here and there was not no one touched his trousers nobody examined them or anything. His pants were just hanging there.

Q – Nobody examined them?
A – No, sir.
Q – Did you feel his trousers?
A – No, sir.
Q – So you don't now whether they were wet or dry?
A – No, sir, and nobody else.
Q – Nobody touched them?
A – No, sir.
Q – Naturally you are very much interested in this lawsuit?
A – Yes, and while I am I am just as pure as gold.
Q – You are a member of the church?
A – Yes, sir.
Q – How long have you been?
A – For since fifty years I have occupied all positions in the church except a deacon and possibly a bishop. I am as pure as gold and I have as good a record as any man you ever looked into the face of.
Q – Was Maurice in business before he was arrested?
A – This time?
Q – Yes.
A – Yes, sir.
Q – How have you been getting your support?
Mr. Houk objected to the question.
The court ruled the question immaterial.
Defense Attorney Cates said he desired to ask if Maurice had been supporting him. The court again ruled the question immaterial. Attorney Cates continued:
Q – Was there any mud on his shoes?
A – No, sir, I seen none and nobody else did.
Hayes was then recross-examined by Mr. Houk:
Q – Did you look at them?

A – Yes, sir, I was right there and seen him scraping them with his nails and I said, 'There is no mud on his shoes" and he said, 'I am trying to scrape them"he said, 'trying to see the number or get the size."

Q – Why didn't you testify about it on the other trial?

A – I was not asked. The thing was so hot before nobody asked anything hardly.

Q – Well, it made a pretty good record for nobody to be asked anything.

A – I didn't make any record.

Q – I say it was a pretty good record for nobody to be asked anything?

A – Well, I don't know about that.

The elder Hayes was then excused from the witness stand.

# BEYOND THE END

Even in death the body of Maurice Hayes still caused controversy. When Will Hayes decided to go to Nashville to claim it and hold the funeral in Knoxville, his action brought a storm of protests from many of the local black leadership. Some expressed the opinion that Hayes's request to be buried in Nashville should be honored.

They also opined that if the body were to be brought there it should be buried on the first day it arrived with simple services. A committee had met to suggest that the funeral be held on Saturday afternoon, March 18, 1922.

Obviously, the committee remembered the chaos of the riot some thirty months before and feared more of the same, or desecration of the body. But circumstances would not allow for a quick funeral.

Mr. Hayes accompanied Maurice's body from Nashville and arrived on Thursday, March 16. He announced that the funeral would be held on Sunday, March 19, at Logan Temple. When the pastor informed him that he would be away from the city to fill another engagement on Sunday, Hayes decided to have the funeral on Monday, the 20th.

Long before the funeral cortege arrived, the spacious auditorium of the church was filled to capacity. Not a seat was available. When the body reached the church, it was impossible to get standing room and it became necessary to take the casket and family in through the side door of the church.

After the body was placed in front of the altar, five white men filed passed the casket, one of whom was dressed in overalls. Several other white people were in attendance.

During the wake at the Hayes home on Campbell Street, there had been a continual line of marchers into the home—white and black, women and children, who went there to look on the remains of the young man who had been electrocuted at the Nashville State Prison. Some walked, some came on horseback, and some came in buggies.

The body reposed in a beautiful lavender casket and was dressed in a robe, all of which were a gift of Elder Preston Taylor, well-known Nashville businessman and undertaker. A wig was used on Hayes's head to take the place of his hair which was shaved off prior to his electrocution.

At the funeral, Logan Temple Pastor Reverend T.H. Medford, was somewhat handicapped due to the conspicuous absence of other pastors who suddenly found other places to be. He called on Reverend C.C. Ellis and another new pastor, who prayed and read an original poem that was sent to be read at the services.

The pastor read an obituary that had been written by professor Ambrose Caliver, a former Knoxvillian and teacher at Fisk University in Nashville. Miss Sylvia Kidd, a Knoxville schoolteacher, sang a solo.

Reverend Medford then rose to deliver one of the shortest eulogies on record. Said he:

\* \* \*

> *There is no person within the sound of my voice, but who is thoroughly acquainted with the facts in connection with this occasion, and as the press of the city has so clearly given the accounts in detail, there is little more that can be said. You have heard the obituary as was written by the Nashville professor, which tells you more of the attitude of the deceased, prior to his death. I will now ask that the undertaker take charge.*

At the request of the family, the casket was opened and the ushers directed the large crowd to file passed and review the remains. As Mrs. Hayes looked at the face of her son for the last time, she fainted, and required the attention of a physician to revive her.

Although Hayes had attended Logan Temple A.M.E. Zion Church as a youngster, he had never been properly baptized. Realizing the end might be near, he asked one of his frequent visitors to the jail, Reverend S.L. McDowell of the First Baptist Church of Nashville, to baptize him.

Since this was contrary to Reverend McDowell's faith, he called in Reverend F.J. Smith who administered the service of baptism as Hayes desired.

Hayes had lived a carefree, precarious life. He suffered a senseless, needless death at the hands of a system which could not tolerate his lifestyle lifestyle of race mixing which had brought him into the world, and ironically, removed him from it.

# Ex-Mayor McCulloch Commits Suicide

After the death of Maurice in the electric chair, John McCulloch, his biological father, felt a heavy blow in the pit of his stomach. Though he could never publicly recognize Maurice as his son and could never overtly indicate such to be true, in his heart he had a deep affection for his offspring. Maurice was the only child he had. Although he and his wife had been married for twenty-two years, they had no children.

Although McCulloch was a portly man, there was an interesting resemblance between him and Maurice. The shape of their heads was the same, their hair texture was the same, and were it not for the chubbiness of McCulloch's face, there would have been a real likeness there, too.

Ironically, during the city elections of 1919, when McCulloch was seeking reelection as Knoxville's mayor, Maurice was arrested for the murder of Bertha Langley. There were whispers that Mayor McCulloch would be exposed. Just two days before the election on September 6, 1919, the Knoxville Journal stated, "There was more than a hint that a sensational charge would be made openly within a few days."

Many in the black community believed these threats against

the mayor referred to his relationship to Maurice Hayes. But nothing came of the threat. In fact, no sensational charge was ever made.

Four years after Maurice had been sent to the electric chair, McCulloch still had his moments of disbelief. On Wednesday, June 30, 1926, he attended the board meeting of the Second National Bank, where the directors announced that the bank was celebrating its most prosperous year since its founding in 1887. Much praise was heaped on McCulloch for his leadership as president in the growth of the bank. But McCulloch really did not feel like celebrating.

At fifty-seven, he had been suffering for some time from the complications of diabetes. He was greatly concerned about the treatments that had been prescribed by his doctor. He was not sure he could bear the rigors of such treatment.

He remained through the board meeting, but shortly after he bade his associates adieu and left the bank early, indicating that he was not feeling well. He decided to walk home believing the exercise would do him good. After all, his home was just a few blocks away.

As McCulloch left his office that afternoon in mental and physical misery from his affliction, he reminisced about his days as a young man and about his successes in government and private life. One of his thoughts was of Maurice and how he enjoyed watching him as a young boy when his foster mother, Hazel Hayes, brought him to work with her at the home of his cousin, Henry McFarland. How he enjoyed watching the handsome three-year-old frolic through the house.

Of course, it was his suggestion that the boy be brought to the McFarland home when he had some free time to be there. He delighted in having the boy sit on his knee and tweak his nose.

He enjoyed feeding him and fussing over him when he took a nap on the pallet on the floor.

McCulloch offered no explanation to Mrs. Hayes for asking her to bring Maurice with her and she sought none. In her heart, she knew. Although most of the extra money she received for the welfare of Maurice came through the McFarlands, on occasion McCulloch could not resist the urge to hand her money to buy the boy one thing or another.

As McCulloch continued his seven-block walk down Gay Street on the way home, he tipped his hat to several ladies who paused to speak to him. He shook hands and slapped the back of a dozen or so men who greeted him. It was a great remedy for any politician, no matter what the ailment.

Although the walk itself was a relatively short one, Gay Street was a very busy place with nearly crowded sidewalks and scores of busy shops and movie theaters. On the one hand, he could smell the fresh popcorn as he passed the McClellan five-and-ten-cent store. Just as strong was the aroma of flowers from Baum's Florist across the street.

He looked at the marquees at the Strand and Majestic theaters. He thought of all those businesses he had helped to attract to Knoxville. He was pleased that his bank had lent money to expand and develop some of them.

As he crossed Vine Avenue near the site of the greatest skirmish during the riot of 1919, he again thought of Maurice. He envisioned him as the dapper young man who often stood on the corner of Vine and Central chatting with his friends. He remembered that one of Maurice's last efforts on that corner was to deliver poll tax receipts to those who had registered to vote in his last run for mayor.

And he could also see Maurice at an earlier time when he

was a teenager full of pranks. When Maurice came to him as a teen to run errands, he loved to tousle the young man's hair. He really didn't need Maurice as an errand boy, but it was an excuse to see him and to give him money. Maurice was always appreciative and genuinely liked McCulloch.

On his walk, McCulloch crossed Jackson Avenue and started across the grand Gay Street Bridge, which had been initiated during his administration as mayor. Boy, was he proud of that structure! He looked down at the passing steam engine pulling a string of freight cars. He remembered the days before the bridge when pedestrians and horse-and-buggy riders had to stop as the train went by. Now, Gay Street had been raised and all traffic crossed over the bridge.

At the corner of Depot and Gay he saw a couple he knew leaving the Southern Railway Depot. He chatted with them briefly before heading toward the Astor Café owned by the Regas Brothers. By the time he crossed Magnolia Avenue, his pain and misery had taken a turn for the worse. His vision was blurry and his kidneys were in excruciating pain. He did not want his wife to know how bad it was and decided not to let on.

He finally made it to Fifth Avenue, just a half block from his residence and heaved a sigh of relief. The walk he thought would be good for him had turned into an ordeal.

The McCullochs lived in a spacious apartment house directly across the street from Knoxville High School, which had been erected in 1910. He climbed the steps and opened the door.

He chatted briefly with his wife and suggested that he would feel better if he had some ice cream. As Mrs. McCulloch left the room to fill his request, he began to undress. Before she could return, he pulled a pistol from the chest of drawers, held it to his right temple, and pulled the trigger. The bullet passed through the left side of his head.

Mrs. McCulloch heard the shot and rushed to him as he lay in a pool of blood on the floor. She summoned his personal physician, Dr. Amos Milburn, and immediately phoned the bank to inform his colleagues. Several of them arrived shortly after the doctor. As word spread, a crowd began to swell around the home of the popular banker.

McCulloch lay in a coma from 3:15 p.m. Wednesday until 11:00 p.m. Thursday night. Doctors at his bedside had detected no voluntary movement or action on the part of the stricken man. Earlier in the day, his pulse quickened followed by laborious respiration.

It had been suggested by some in the medical community that his life might be prolonged by an operation to drain and clean the head wound. It was also suggested that all odds were against a recovery and Mrs. McCulloch, almost prostrate with grief, vetoed the proposal. After nearly thirty-two hours, McCulloch slipped into eternity.

The body was taken to the E.B. Mann Mortuary at 404 West Church Street to be prepared for burial. On Friday, at 2:00 p.m., the body was moved back to the McCulloch residence on Fifth Avenue for the wake. Scores of citizens, both black and white, filed past the casket during the afternoon and into the night.

On July 2, 1926, the *Knoxville Journal* said of McCulloch:
   . . . *John E. is dead.*

Conveying that no more need to be implied than those four words.

*Few men who have trod the stage of life of a municipality*

*had a surer grip on the affections of as many people of all races and creeds as the dead banker.*

*Hundreds, probably upwards in the thousands, of calls have been made by telephone to inquire as to his condition, and a constant stream of people passed through West Fifth Avenue and Central Street throughout the day yesterday hoping against hope for a message of hope from the apartment room where McCulloch was entering the last sleep.*

McCulloch first ran for mayor of Knoxville in 1911 and was defeated by popular incumbent Mayor Samuel G. Heiskell, who had served four terms prior to the 1911 elections. He was elected to his first term in 1915 and again in 1917. He was seeking a third term during the heat of Red Summer.

His opponent in the 1919 election was E.W. Neal, who attacked McCulloch for not spending enough time in his mayoral duties. He took McCulloch to task for the great indebtedness of the city and Neal advocated that all teachers, male and female, should receive the same pay (this discussion did not include black teachers). He also believed that teachers should be under civil service and that all city employees should work an eight-hour day.

McCulloch, on the other hand, appealed directly to women who would be voting for the first time in city elections. He called for a mass meeting at the Market House and invited 'Good people to hear the truth the good women of Knoxville are especially invited. One entire section of seats on the main floor of the hall has been reserved for the ladies and their escorts."

McCulloch also claimed that he was not in favor of forced annexation, which brought people into the city limits against their will. He and Neal had varying arguments about the construction of the Gay Street Bridge over the Southern Railway tracks.

In greater Knoxville there were 6,831 women registered to vote. The unknown quantity was whether they would vote independently or in line with their husbands or other relatives.

On September 7, 1919, the day after the election, the *Knoxville Journal* headlines declared: "Neal Is Victor In Close Race; Wins Over McCulloch By Less Than 500." The female vote was evenly divided. Neal received a total of 6,806 votes and McCulloch received 6,307. He was beaten in the suburban wards which were not a part of the city when he was first elected. He carried the old wards by a 700-vote majority.

So, just one week after the upheaval of Knoxville's Red Summer, the popular mayor went down to defeat and returned fulltime to his banking business.

There were no newspaper editorials to really dissect the election and to reach a deep conclusion for McCulloch's defeat. There seemed to be no hint that the heat of Red Summer aided his downfall. Ironically, the *Crisis* Magazine of April 1919 carried a positive note of his attitude in race relations:

*'An ill day will arrive if there is a revival of racial animosity in the South,'* said McCulloch.

# NOTES BEYOND THE END

Even today, eighty-one years after the initial event, there are lingering questions about Maurice Hayes and the race riot: Who actually committed the murder of Mrs. Langley? How many people were killed during the shooting? Was the white mayor really Maurice's father?

There are stories of bodies of riot victims being stacked in an icehouse. There is the story of uncovering a mass grave of riot victims during the construction of the City/County Building in the late 1970s. There are those who swear that certain newspapers carrying the stories have disappeared.

*The older the story gets, the more is added to the facts. Even newcomers to the city have versions of what happened. One intriguing revelation appeared in the October 1927 issue of the NAACP Crisis Magazine which discussed the Hayes case in an article titled The Terrible Truth:*

*We must not allow ourselves to forget a far less widely known case. August 29, 1919, Maurice Hayes of Knoxville, Tennessee was arrested and charged with the murder of a white woman, Mrs. Bertha Langley. On October 4th, he was convicted of murder in the first degree. 'There was no charge to the jury* in sentencing him. The court was prejudiced to such an extent that the trial judge would not or did not hear witnesses for the defense.' The police were against Hayes because he had been 'in politics.' The community wanted to lynch him.

The case was appealed to the Tennessee Supreme Court and heard in January 1920. The judgment of the lower court was set aside on a technicality (that the execution date was on a Sunday) and Hayes was tried again in April, 1921.

He brought in witnesses to establish a complete alibi, nevertheless, he was again found guilty of murder in the first degree and ordered to be executed June 26, 1921. The case was again appealed, but the state Supreme Court upheld the lower court and set the execution for December 15th. On December 14th, through the efforts of the NAACP and his friends, a respite of ninety days was granted.

Commutation of the sentence to life imprisonment was asked, but it was all in vain. On March 15, 1922, Maurice Hayes was executed.

Six years later, in August 1927, the chief of police of Norton, Virginia, informed the Knoxville authorities that Mrs. Sadie Mendil, a white woman of twenty-eight, had confessed to the murder of Mrs. Langley.

Her name at the time was Mrs. John Roddy and she lived at Devonia, Tennessee. Dressed in men's clothes and with her face blackened, according to her story, she slipped into the Langley woman's home and killed her in bed. She did so, she said, because a few nights previous she had trailed her husband, a traveling man, to the Langley home, and had seen her husband and the Langley woman together.

Mrs. Mendil, despite her confession, was released because the record showed 'no charge against the woman.' Maurice

*Hayes had borne that charge to his grave, because he was a Negro 'in politics.'*

Somehow, even the *Crisis* had missed the real lesson of Southern justice.

# ABOUT THE AUTHOR

Robert J. Booker was born in Knoxville, Tennessee, April 4, 1935. He graduated from Austin High School in 1953. He spent three years in the U.S. Army in France and England as an information education specialist. In 1962 he graduated from Knoxville College where he majored in English and minored in French. At Knoxville College he was two-term president of the student body and spent the summer of 1961 in Guinea West Africa in Operation Crossroads Africa. As a student leader he helped to initiate and conduct the sit-in movement in Knoxville to desegregate downtown lunch counters and movie theaters. During his freshman year he was elected president of the campus chapter of the NAACP.

In 1967 Booker became the first black ever elected from Knoxville to the State Legislature. He was elected to three terms serving until 1972.

Booker served a total of seven years as administrative assistant to Mayor Kyle Testerman of Knoxville. He was appointed by Governor Lamar Alexander as the first black ever to serve on the Tennessee Civil Service Commission.

Booker was executive director of the Beck Cultural Exchange Center for seventeen years. He is the historian for the Beck Cultural Exchange Center, Knoxville College and Tabernacle Baptist Church. He is the founding president of the National Austin High School Alumni Association. From 1987 to 1991 he wrote a weekly column for the old Knoxville Journal and since 2003, he has written a weekly column for the Knoxville News Sentinel.

For the past thirty-eight years Booker has done extensive research on the history of Knoxville and has authored numerous publications including: 'The Story of Mechanicsville 1875-2008" and 'The Story of East Knoxville from the Beginning 1856-2004." His books include: The re-release of 'The Heat of a Red Summer, Race Mixing, Race Rioting in 1919 Knoxville," 'Two Hundred Years of Black Culture in Knoxville, Tennessee 1791-1991,"'"And There Was Light! The 120-Year History of Knoxville College Knoxville, Tennessee 1875-1995,'"'An Encyclopedia: Experiences of Black People in Knoxville, Tennessee 1844-1974," and 'From the Bottom Up."

# BECK CULTURAL EXCHANGE CENTER

### African American History & Culture
*Established 1975*
1927 Dandridge Avenue
Knoxville, Tennessee 37915
(865) 524-8461 | BeckCenter.net

Beck —Beck is a nonprofit 501(c)(3) organization that was established in 1975 as a result of Knoxville's Urban Renewal projects. The Urban Renewal projects began in 1959 under Title I of the Housing Act of 1949. The projects relocated and displaced many black families and businesses. Much of the heritage of the black community was erased from the map. Except for one or two structures in the city and the historic buildings at Knoxville College, edifices that once stood as monuments to the struggles of early leaders no longer exist. Absent of the establishment of Beck, these places and the people may never have existed.

Beck is the only organization in the region dedicated to local and regional African American history and culture. Beck is the storehouse of African American history and culture and has been designated by the state as a primary repository of black history and culture in East Tennessee.

## BECK VISION

To be the desired place that people go to learn, discover and experience the rich legacy of African Americans inside a vibrant Cultural Corridor.

## BECK MISSION

To be the place where African American history and culture are preserved, nurtured, taught, & continued.

## JAMES AND ETHEL BECK

Beck is named in honor of James Garfield (1881-1969) and Ethel Benson (1897- 1970) Beck. James and Ethel were two of the most glamorous and influential members of the black community in Knoxville during the period of the 1920s- 1960s and were the last people to live in the Beck mansion. Funds from the Beck Estate were used to establish the Beck Cultural Exchange Center.

**BECK IS CRAFTING A VIBRANT CULTURAL CORRIDOR IN KNOXVILLE**